ANTON CHEKHOV

The Cherry Orchard

translated from the Russian by
MICHAEL FRAYN

with commentary and notes by
NICK WORRALL

Bloomsbury Methuen Drama
An imprint of Bloomsbury Publishing Plc

BLOOMSBURY
LONDON · OXFORD · NEW YORK · NEW DELHI · SYDNEY

Bloomsbury Methuen Drama
An imprint of Bloomsbury Publishing Plc

Imprint previously known as Methuen Drama

50 Bedford Square	1385 Broadway
London	New York
WC1B 3DP	NY 10018
UK	USA

www.bloomsbury.com

BLOOMSBURY, METHUEN DRAMA and the Diana logo are trademarks of
Bloomsbury Publishing Plc

This edition first published in Great Britain in 1995 by Methuen Drama
Reissued with additional material and a new cover design, 2005
Revised and reissued with a new cover, 2009
Reprinted by Bloomsbury Methuen Drama 2014 (twice), 2016

This translation first published in Great Britain in 1978
by Eyre Methuen Ltd; reprinted in a revised edition in 1988 by Methuen London Ltd

Translation © 1978, 1988, 1990 by Michael Frayn
Translator's Introduction © 1978, 1988, 1990 by Michael Frayn
Commentary and Notes © 1995, 2005, 2009 by Methuen Drama

British Library Cataloguing-in-Publication Data
A catalogue record for this book is available from the British Library.

ISBN: PB: 978-0-4136-9500-0

Library of Congress Cataloging-in-Publication Data
A catalog record for this book is available from the Library of Congress.

Series: Student Editions

Typeset by Wilmaset Ltd, Birkenhead, Wirral

Contents

Anton Chekhov: 1860–1904

1860 Born, the grandson of a serf and third son of the merchant grocer Pavel Yegorovich Chekhov and his wife Yevgeniya Yakovlevna Morozova, in Taganrog, a small southern port on the Sea of Azov, where he spends his first nineteen years.

1868 Enters the local *gimnaziya* or high school, where he acquires a reputation as a practical joker and is known as 'bomb-head' because of the overdeveloped size of his cranium.

1876 His father, bankrupt, flees from Taganrog concealed beneath a mat at the bottom of a cart. The family follow him to Moscow, leaving Chekhov behind to complete his schooling. Chekhov writes a short (2–3 pages) 'absurd' play, called *A Forced Declaration or The Sudden Death of a Horse, or The Magnanimity of the Russian People*.

1878 He writes a full-length play, and a vaudeville, *Why the Hen Clucks*, both now lost. The play, *Bezottsovshchina* (Fatherless/Without Patrimony) may be the one which later resurfaced, and is generally known as *Platonov*.

1879 Having completed his education, Chekhov moves to Moscow to join his family, now impoverished and living in a red-light district. He enters the medical faculty of Moscow University where he studies for the next five years.

1880 Begins contributing humorous stories to minor magazines under the pen-name, Antosha Chekhonte. His first short stories are published in the tenth issue of the magazine *Strekoza* (The Dragonfly).

1880 Chekhov writes for Moscow and St Petersburg comic
 –87 magazines under various pseudonyms, 'A Doctor without Patients', 'A Man without a Spleen', 'My Brother's Brother', and others.

1881 He offers a full-length play to the Moscow Maly Theatre which is rejected. Presumed lost, a play is discovered in 1920, without a title, but containing plot elements which resemble those of the rejected work. It is most usually known as *Platonov*, after the play's central character. Because of its inordinate length, the play is usually acted in adapted or abbreviated versions – the most famous being Michael Frayn's *Wild Honey* (1984).

1884 Chekhov qualifies as a doctor and begins practising in the Moscow regions of Zvenigorod and Voskresensk – the start of a sporadic second career which, over the years, brings him much hard work and little income. Describing the relationship between his work as a doctor and that as a writer, he compares them to those between a man and his wife and a man and his mistress, respectively. His first collection of stories, *Fairy Tales of Melpomene*, is published, as is a three-page 'terrible-awful-disgraceful desperate t-r-r-rragedy', *Dishonourable Tragedians and Leprous Dramatists*. A 'dramatic study in one act', *On The High Road*, is rejected by the censor as 'a gloomy and sordid play'. He begins to show first signs of the tubercular condition which was to end his life twenty years later.

1885 Makes his first trip to St Petersburg where he meets and befriends Alexey Suvorin, millionaire proprietor of the newspaper *Novoye vremya* (The New Time), a man of reactionary views who has a concession on all the railway bookstalls in Russia.

1886 Begins writing for *Novoye vremya*. His second collection of short stories, *Motley Tales*, is published. He also writes two short one-acters – *Swan Song* and *On the Harmfulness of Tobacco*.

1887 First production of a full-length play, *Ivanov*, given on 19 November at the Korsh Theatre in Moscow. Despite only four rehearsals 'the play had a substantial success' with curtain calls after each act including one, following Act Two, for the author himself. The production was also hissed. According to Chekhov, the second performance '. . . didn't go badly . . . Again there were curtain calls after Act Three (twice) and after Act Four, but no hisses this time' (Letters to his brother, Alexander, dated 20 and 24 November 1887).

1888 Writes a long short story, 'The Steppe', which appears in one of the prestigious 'thick journals' *Russkaya mysl'* (Russian Thought) and which marks a change in Chekhov's attitude to his fiction writing, thanks largely to an appreciative letter from the literary critic, D. V. Grigorovich. Henceforth, Chekhov will write fewer stories and, generally, longer and more substantial ones. This year also sees the appearance of his best-known and most performed one-act 'jokes' – *The Bear* and *The Proposal*. At the première of the first, a samovar bursts on stage and scalds one of the actors. The Russian Academy awards Chekhov the Pushkin prize for a book of short stories, *In the Twilight*.

1889 Chekhov's full-length play, *The Wood Demon*, strongly influenced by Tolstoyan ideas, opens at the Abramova Theatre in Moscow but closes after only three performances. It will later reappear, in revised form, as *Uncle Vanya*. He writes two more short plays, *A Tragedian in Spite of Himself* and the more extended *The Wedding*.

1890 Sets out on a journey in unsprung carts over unsurfaced roads, as well as by train and steamer, to the convict settlement on the island of Sakhalin off Russia's eastern seaboard. The journey takes from 21 April to 11 July. Once there, Chekhov conducts a census of some 10,000 convicts, averaging 160 interviews a day as part of a three-month medical/statistical survey which includes the examination of living conditions among convicts and exiles, looking at school and library provision, etc. He also makes travel notes which are written up as nine articles for *Novoye vremya* and which become the basis of the documentary work, *The Island of Sakhalin*, published in 1895. He leaves Siberia on 13 October and returns by sea via Hong Kong (where he admires British colonial rule) and Ceylon (where he admires the beauty of the women), arriving in Odessa via the recently opened Suez Canal on 1 December.

1891 His one-act play *The Anniversary* staged. Makes his first trip to Western Europe in the company of Suvorin.

1892 He purchases an estate near Moscow, Melikhovo (now a Chekhov museum, as is his residence-cum-surgery in Moscow), where he and the remainder of his family move. During the course of this and the following year, Chekhov immerses himself in the struggle against the effects on the local population of famine and cholera. He also helps to build schools, plants fruit trees, cultivates fir, pine, larch and oak, grows flowers, stocks fishponds, and runs the estate as a self-supporting commune growing its own cereal and vegetables. His medical 'diocese' covers 26 villages. One of his best-known short stories, 'Ward 6', is published in November.

1894 His health worsens but, despite this, he travels to Europe again in the company of Suvorin.

1895 Chekhov's fame as a writer spreads. He meets Tolstoy for the first time.

1896 Sponsors the construction of a primary school in nearby Talezh. *The Seagull* is premièred unsuccessfully at the Aleksandrinsky Theatre, St Petersburg. Chekhov vows never to write another play.

1897 Sponsors construction of a primary school in the neighbouring village of Novosyolki. Suffers a violent lung haemorrhage while dining with Suvorin and is diagnosed as suffering from tuberculosis. He is also plagued by piles, gastritis, migraine, dizzy spells, and palpitations of the heart (not unlike the comic protagonist, Lomov, in his one-act 'joke' *The Proposal*). A collection of his plays is published which includes *Uncle Vanya*.

1897 Wintering in Nice for his health, he becomes interested in the
–98   Dreyfus case and takes Zola's side in defence of the French officer. Relations cool with the rather anti-semitic Suvorin.

1898 Has a villa built in Yalta on the Black Sea (now a Chekhov museum) where weather conditions are better suited for his illness. Following the opening of the Moscow Art Theatre in October 1898, *The Seagull* is given its second, successful, première in December, produced by Stanislavsky and Nemirovich-Danchenko and with Olga Knipper as Arkadina and Stanislavsky as Trigorin.

1899 Sells Melikhovo and moves permanently to Yalta. Also sells the copyright on all his works, past, present and future, to the St Petersburg publisher, A. F. Marks, for 75,000 roubles. *Uncle Vanya* staged with tremendous success by the Moscow Art Theatre on 26 October, with Knipper as Yelena and Stanislavsky as Astrov. Chekhov begins corresponding with Knipper, whom he had admired at a rehearsal of *Tsar Fedor* in 1898 and whom he is to marry in 1901. One of his best-known short stories, 'Lady with Lapdog', is published. Having corresponded with Gorky, Chekhov meets him for the first time and is instrumental in getting the Art Theatre to perform Gorky's plays *The Merchant Class* and *The Lower Depths.*

1899–1902 Edits and publishes his *Complete Works* in eleven volumes.

1900 Elected to honorary membership of the Academy of Sciences. Works on *Three Sisters* with members of the Moscow Art Theatre in mind. Winters in Nice.

1901 *Three Sisters* premièred at the Art Theatre on 31 January with Knipper as Masha and Stanislavsky as Vershinin. A qualified success. On 25 May he marries Knipper and honeymoons in south-east Russia. Meetings with Leo Tolstoy, Maxim Gorky, Ivan Bunin and Alexander Kuprin.

1902 Resigns from the Academy of Sciences in protest at Gorky's expulsion from that institution for his radical beliefs.

1903 Second edition of his *Complete Works* published. Despite worsening health, he works on his final play, *The Cherry Orchard*, again with specific Moscow Art Theatre actors in mind.

1904 Première of *The Cherry Orchard* on 17 January. Chekhov is taken seriously ill in the spring. He and Knipper leave for the health resort of Badenweiler in the Black Forest area of Germany, where he dies on 2 July. His last words are a request for champagne. His body is brought by rail to Moscow in a waggon for frozen goods marked 'Oysters' and, on 9 July is interred in the cemetery of the Novodevichy Monastery, where many of Russia's great writers lie.

Plot

A sequence of unfortunate events, including the death of her husband followed by the accidental death by drowning of her seven-year-old son, has driven Lyubov Ranyevskaya from her Russian estate to seek consolation abroad. She has been pursued to France by her Russian lover, with whom she has been living for the past five years in Menton and Paris, but has now been abandoned by him. Her daughter, Anya, accompanied by her eccentric governess, Charlotta, has travelled on a rescue mission to Paris where Lyubov has been living in straitened circumstances on the proceeds of the sale of the Menton estate, most of which has been squandered by her lover. The Russian estate, meanwhile, has been ineffectually run in her absence by Ranyevskaya's brother, Gayev, a feckless middle-aged aristocrat with a passion for billiards and boiled sweets. He has been aided by Ranyevskaya's nun-like foster-daughter, Varya, and a maid, Dunyasha, who suffers from 'nerves', and a clumsy estate-clerk, Yepikhodov, who affects a manner of 'educated' speech. Also in charge of the estate is a semi-senile eighty-seven-year-old family retainer, Firs, for whom time has stopped in 1861, the year of the emancipation of the serfs, which he refers to as the 'disaster'. Also associated with the estate are a rich merchant and former peasant, Lopakhin, whose family were once employed here as serfs, and whose possible marriage to Varya is frequently mooted, and who has a plan for saving the estate. A neighbouring landowner, Simeonov-Pishchik, and an 'eternal' student, Trofimov, complete the group. The former seems in thrall to his daughter, Dashenka, and is constantly borrowing money; the latter was tutor to the drowned son, Grisha, and anticipating Ranyevskaya's arrival, has returned to the estate from his wanderings and taken up residence in an outside bath-house. He is in love with Anya, his junior by at least ten years.

The play opens on the cold spring morning of Ranyevskaya's return, accompanied by her Frenchified, ill-mannered Russian manservant, Yasha, and escorted by Anya and Charlotta. Although

the return seems a permanent one, we soon learn that
Ranyevskaya's lover has been bombarding her with telegrams
appealing for forgiveness and begging her to come back to him.
Her return to Paris at the end of the play is finally precipitated by
the sale of the estate and its famous cherry orchard, which has long
been unproductive, badly managed and is now mortgaged to the
hilt.

Act One

The curtain rises on the former nursery. It is two o'clock in the
morning and almost first light. The cherry trees are in blossom
although outside it is still cold and frosty. Gayev, Varya and
Simeonov-Pishchik have gone to the nearby railway station to meet
Ranyevskaya. Lopakhin, who intended going, has fallen asleep
over a book. Dunyasha bustles about excitedly. Yepikhodov arrives
wearing squeaky new boots and bearing a bunch of flowers for the
newcomers, which he promptly drops, before knocking over a
piece of furniture.
  Offstage noise heralds the arrival of the travelling party. Servants
bearing their luggage cross the stage, preceded by Firs in full livery
and followed by Charlotta and the others. She has a small dog on a
lead which, she claims, 'eats nuts', much to Simeonov-Pishchik's
delight. Realising she is in the old nursery, Ranyevskaya is moved
to recollections of her childhood. Anya describes the melancholy
conditions of her mother's Parisian lifestyle but exclaims excitedly
that, whilst there, she '. . . went up in a balloon!' Dunyasha is
impressed with Yasha and his acquisition of 'French' sophistication
since she last saw him. He snatches a kiss with arrogant
boorishness. Firs assumes the role of major-domo, serving coffee
with white gloves, whilst Gayev rehearses imaginary billiard shots
(something which he continues to do throughout the play).
Lopakhin proposes a plan to save the estate but brother and sister
will have none of it since the scheme would involve cutting down
the cherry orchard. Varya unlocks the glass doors of a large
bookcase which contains some telegrams from Paris, prompting
Gayev to deliver a birthday address to this remarkable piece of
furniture which, it turns out, is one hundred years old. Dawn has

broken, revealing the orchard in all its beauty, evoking memories of the past and images of Ranyevskaya's dead mother.

Trofimov enters and is embraced by Ranyevskaya who weeps in remembrance of her dead son. She is also depressed by Trofimov's changed, shoddy appearance. Mention is made, in passing, of a rich great-aunt who might be able to help save the estate. Gayev suggests the possibility of borrowing money from the bank. The sun is now fully up and Firs, who still treats Gayev like a small boy, urges him to go to bed. Varya leads the sleepy Anya to her room. The sound of a shepherd's pipe is heard in the distance and Trofimov, alone on the sunlit stage, describes Anya in semi-rapturous terms as 'My sunshine! My springtime!'

Act Two

Act Two is set in the open countryside a month or so later. There is evidence that the spot was once a wayside shrine, while signs of the modern world are visible in a row of telegraph poles receding towards a dimly distant town. Yepikhodov, Charlotta, Yasha and Dunyasha have gathered here towards dusk. Yepikhodov strums a guitar and threatens suicide out of unrequited love for Dunyasha, who flirts with Yasha who, in turn, flaunts his cosmopolitan *savoir-faire*. Charlotta incongruously munches a cucumber, whilst toting a shotgun and bemoaning her indeterminate identity and her orphaned childhood. Yepikhodov wonders why Fate constantly buffets him, causing spiders to crawl on his chest and beetles to drop in his drink.

Ranyevskaya, Gayev and Lopakhin arrive. Time is running out for the estate but the two aristocrats refuse to give the merchant a straight answer to the 'vulgar' suggestion of leasing the land for summer cottages. Ranyevskaya mentions that she attempted suicide in France when her lover abandoned her and suggests Lopakhin marry Varya – to which he agrees, but without enthusiasm. Gayev says he's been offered a job in a bank. Firs arrives with his master's coat against the encroaching cold. Anya and Trofimov arrive. The latter rhapsodises about mankind's future and condemns the Russian intelligentsia. Lopakhin thinks Russians should be giants commensurate with the scale of their country, while Ranyevskaya comforts herself with the reassuring prospect of the very ordinary Yepikhodov who traverses the stage strumming his guitar.

A lull ensues during which Gayev delivers a prosaic declamatory address to the setting sun and is told, not for the first time, to keep quiet. A distant sound, like a breaking string, startles them all and is variously and inconclusively interpreted by the four male members of the group. The women are further startled by the sudden appearance out of the wood in the gathering dusk of a tipsy passer-by on his way to the station, who engages in a spot of opportunistic begging. Prompted by fear and guilt, Ranyevskaya gives him a gold coin as Varya takes fright and is disparagingly told by Lopakhin, misquoting Hamlet, to go to a monastery.

The group departs, with Lopakhin's reminder that the sale of the estate is imminent. Anya and Trofimov are left alone and she is treated to one of his sermons, the theme of which is that the past can only be redeemed by suffering and work, and that happiness is approaching. Moonrise is accompanied by the sad notes of Yepikhodov's guitar and the cries of Varya who has come looking for Anya.

Act Three

A party is being given in the house on the day of the sale of the estate. Lopakhin and Gayev have spent the day travelling to and from the auction, which is being held in town, and have not yet returned. The latter has taken with him the hopelessly inadequate sum of 15,000 roubles lent by the great-aunt to purchase the property in her name. To the accompaniment of a small Jewish orchestra, a motley group of guests are dancing and a permanent game of billiards can be heard offstage. Trofimov teases Varya, Ranyevskaya worries about Gayev, Pishchik quotes Nietzsche in support of forgery, and Charlotta practises card tricks, disappearing tricks and throws her voice, much to everyone's amusement. A quarrel between Trofimov and Ranyevskaya on the subject of 'love' ends with Trofimov storming off petulantly and then falling down stairs. The stationmaster recites a poem; the couples dance, and Charlotta can be glimpsed clowning in the background, dressed in a top hat and checked trousers. Lopakhin and Gayev return, the latter soulfully dangling two packages of

herring and anchovies from his hand. Lopakhin announces that he
himself has bought the estate for 90,000 roubles plus the arrears
and celebrates this fact in an ecstasy of unbelief, tinged with
sadness. Varya hurls the bunch of housekeys at her waist to the
floor and exits. Lopakhin summons the band to play whilst he
sadly reproaches Ranyevsksya for not heeding his warnings. Anya
comforts her grief-stricken mother with the prospect of new
orchards to be planted elsewhere.

Act Four

Act Four opens on a cold October day following the August sale.
The weather is fine and sunny – 'good building weather', according
to Lopakhin as he contemplates axing the orchard and
redeveloping the land for summer visitors. The 'nursery' has been
stripped bare except for a few sticks of furniture. Suitcases and
travelling bags hint at imminent departure. Ranyevskaya is
returning to Paris with Yasha; Varya is going to work as a
housekeeper some fifty miles away, unless Lopakhin can be
persuaded to marry her; Trofimov is returning to his university
studies; Gayev is leaving for town and work in the bank,
accompanied, it would seem, by his niece. Charlotta has no clear
idea of where she is heading. Yepikhodov has been retained as
estate clerk by Lopakhin, who is going to Kharkov. Firs is ill and
has gone to hospital (at least so everyone assumes). While waiting
to leave, Yasha drinks almost the entire contents of a bottle of
champagne and Trofimov's departure for the vanguard of Russia's
future is delayed while he tries to find his galoshes. They have
twenty minutes to catch the train which will take them all as far as
the town where they are to go their separate ways. The distant
sound of an axe can be heard. Ranyevskaya informs everyone,
unashamedly, that she intends living in Paris on the money
borrowed from the great-aunt. Pishchik arrives with the good news
that some Englishmen have discovered china clay on his land
which he has leased to them for twenty-four years, and he pays
back some of the money he owes. Ranyevskaya contrives to leave
Lopakhin and Varya alone together in the hope that the former
will propose marriage but, inevitably, nothing comes of it.
Yepikhodov breaks something yet again. Charlotta croons to a

bundle as if it were a baby in swaddling clothes before hurling it to the floor.

Finally, everyone departs, leaving Ranyevskaya and Gayev alone on stage. They embrace and sob quietly as Ranyevskaya bids farewell to her youth and happiness. In contrast, the happy shouts of Anya and Trofimov are heard outside. Finally, the stage is empty and the noise is heard of the external doors being locked. The sound of an axe rings out, followed by the unexpected appearance of Firs, who has not only not been taken to hospital but has been left behind, and is now locked in. He is obviously ill and lies down. Then the sound, like that of a breaking string, is heard again in the distance, dying away. There follows a silence, then the sound of an axe striking a tree somewhere far away as Firs continues to lie motionless on stage.

Commentary

Chekhov and the theatre: general background

Chekhov was active in the theatre at the height of the European
Naturalist movement, the impact of which was felt both in terms
of its philosophy and in its effect on staging practice. A key word
in the vocabulary of the Naturalists was 'determinism'. Under the
influence of those who espoused (and frequently simplified) the
ideas of Charles Darwin, Karl Marx and others, human beings
were seen to be psychologically, physiologically, historically,
economically and environmentally subject to the 'determining'
pressures of heredity and environment, or related to the lower
forms of animal life. The scientific approach to reality and human
affairs which this produced led, in the theatre, to the precise
recreation of ordinary, everyday environments as part of an
attempt to illustrate the way in which people, either individually or
in groups, were shaped by these external pressures. The democratic
criteria of Naturalist ideas (democratic in so far as they embraced
everybody irrespective of class and social standing) also led to an
emphasis on the social norm rather than the social exception
because, if everyone was subject to the same natural laws, it made
little difference whether a dramatic character was of high or low
estate. In fact, the Naturalist movement laid the basis for the
special significance of the latter although, in actual practice,
dramatists tended to concentrate on the lives of the middle classes
rather than those of the 'lower orders'. In his short stories,
Chekhov shows great interest in the lives of ordinary Russian
people, including peasants. In his major plays, however, his interest
is restricted in the main to the milieu of relatively impoverished
gentrified inhabitants of superannuated country estates in the
period following the emancipation of the serfs. Freedom, of sorts,
was given to the Russian peasantry in 1861, the year after
Chekhov was born, his important plays being written between
1887 and 1903.

Naturalism's interest in general scientific laws for human conduct tended to provide a rather reductionist perspective on life, where the 'lowest common denominator', or human average, provided the key to any answers which were available. In dramatic terms, this tended to produce not only a social levelling but a flattening of distinctions between the 'dramatic' and the 'undramatic', the 'significant' and the 'insignificant', the high points of dramatic excitement and the low points of dramatic inactivity. It could even produce an equalisation of the comic and tragic genres, evincing a world in which, as Chekhov said: 'People dine, simply dine and at that moment their happiness is decided or their lives shattered'. He also said that, 'A writer must be as objective as a chemist . . . he must know that dung-heaps play a very respectable part in a landscape . . .'. At its most extreme, this view could even seem to produce a world in which a death was as significant as a yawn or where, as the doctor says in *Three Sisters*, '*Vsyo ravno . . .*' (It's all the same . . .). In other words, there were no significant distinctions or discriminations to be made where there were no longer any meaningfully distinct categories or moral certainties; no blacks or whites, but merely different shades of grey.

Chekhov shared this dramatic landscape with some notable contemporaries all of whom owed debts of varying degrees to the Naturalist movement – including Ibsen, Strindberg, Hauptmann and Shaw. It was also a period during which a previously stagnant phase in European theatre generally, was being countered by a revival of interest in theatre as a serious art form. One consequence was the creation of new playing spaces for the new drama under the aegis of specialised theatre 'directors'. The movement also inspired a new breed of actor, often amateur, but imbued·with the kind of dedication to the art of theatre which the so-called 'professionals' seemed singularly to lack. Such were the examples set by André Antoine and the *Théâtre Libre* in Paris, Otto Brahm and the *Freie Bühne* in Berlin, the German Saxe-Meiningen company who toured Europe extensively, Strindberg's own *Intima Teatren* in Stockholm, J. T. Grein's Independent Theatre and Granville Barker's Court Theatre in London, and Yeats' and Lady Gregory's Abbey Theatre in Dublin. Most influential, as far as Chekhov was concerned, and critical in determining his world-wide

renown as a dramatist, was the creation of the Moscow Art
Theatre by Stanislavsky and Nemirovich-Danchenko, in 1897, and
which between its opening, in October 1898, and the year of
Chekhov's death, in 1904, staged all of his finest plays – *The
Seagull* (1898), *Uncle Vanya* (1899), *Three Sisters* (1901), and
Ivanov (1904).

Naturalist drama in Russia became the almost exclusive preserve
of Maxim Gorky, whose first plays, *The Merchant Class* and *The
Lower Depths* (the latter set in a dosshouse), Chekhov had
encouraged the Art Theatre to stage. Gorky's example had been
anticipated in the work of Leo Tolstoy and others who wrote plays
based on peasant life, of which the most significant was Tolstoy's
own *The Power of Darkness* (1886). Chekhov, too, was aware of
his debt to a Russian dramatic tradition which reached back to
Gogol (in the 1830s), Turgenev (in the 1850s) and to Alexander
Ostrovsky, whose dramatic output extended from *c.*1850 to
*c.*1880. Chekhov's early one-act plays such as *The Bear*, *The
Proposal*, *The Jubilee* and *The Wedding* appear strongly influenced
by farcical and 'grotesque' elements to be found in Gogol's *The
Government Inspector* and *Marriage* as well as in Turgenev's plays
of the 1850s. Act Two of *Ivanov* (the soirée at the Lebedyevs')
seems to combine elements of grotesquerie from both Gogol and
Turgenev, as does Vanya's attempted shooting of Serebryakov in
Act Three of *Uncle Vanya*. The quarrel between Lomov and his
'fiancée', in *The Proposal*, is highly reminiscent of the quarrel
between brother and sister in Turgenev's *Lunch with the Marshal
of the Nobility*, whilst Chekhov's *Wedding* would seem
anticipatory of Act Three of his own *The Cherry Orchard*. In many
respects, Chekhov's plays seem least like the Turgenev play with
which they are frequently compared, *A Month in the Country*,
which has a country estate setting in common but little else.
Neither do they have much in common with the plays of
Ostrovsky, although a play like *Talent and its Admirers*, with its
insight into the world of the nineteenth-century acting profession,
provides very useful background to an understanding of Nina's life
as an actress in *The Seagull*.

Mention of this last play is a reminder of Chekhov's interest in
theatrical movements other than the Naturalist. In many respects,
he may be said to have shared the interest of Konstantin Treplev

(in *The Seagull*) in the pursuit of 'new forms', even if he does not entirely share the young artist's spirit of hostility to Naturalist theatre in general and the way in which it reduces 'high priests in the temple of art' to ordinary mortals who 'eat and drink . . . walk about and wear their suits' in a setting which consists of 'three walls lit by artificial lighting' (trans. Frayn, 1986, p. 5).

Konstantin's play-within-the-play is an early, rather inconclusive attempt to put some of the ideas of the dramatic 'Symbolists' into action. Led by the philosopher Vladimir Solovyov, who influenced the work of Andrey Bely, Alexander Blok, Leonid Andreyev and others in the early 1900s, and inspired by the work of French Symbolist poets and the work of Maurice Maeterlinck, the Russian reaction against the dominance of Naturalism in the theatre was spearheaded by members of the Russian Symbolist movement. Generally speaking, the Symbolists were reacting against the materialistic outlook enshrined in Naturalism and encouraged a resurgence of the idealistic, the aesthetic and the metaphysical. In emphasising the primary validity of 'other worlds', as an aspect of their reaction against materialism, the Symbolists tended to suggest that the one we take for granted is actually insubstantial and unreal. Towards the end of his life, Chekhov himself expressed interest in the work of Maurice Maeterlinck and encouraged the staging of work by the Belgian dramatist. Actor/directors, such as Vsevolod Meyerhold, and poet/novelists, like Andrey Bely, detected 'symbolist' elements in *The Cherry Orchard* (see Meyerhold's essay 'The Naturalistic Theatre and the Theatre of Mood' in E. Braun (ed.) *Meyerhold on Theatre*, 1991, pp. 23–34, and Andrey Bely's essay on *The Cherry Orchard* in L. Senelick (ed.) *Russian Dramatic Theory from Pushkin to the Symbolists*, 1981, pp. 89–92) and Andrey Bely even detected quasi-symbolist elements in a play like *Ivanov* when it was staged by the Moscow Art Theatre in 1904, despite the fact that the play itself dates from the late 1880s. Just as his dramatic output straddled two centuries, Chekhov's drama also spanned a period during which major changes were taking place in the arts. To what extent his drama can then be considered to be Naturalist, Impressionist, Symbolist, Expressionist, Surrealist, or any combination of these, becomes an interesting issue in the debate surrounding the interpretation of his plays.

Playwriting was very much a second string to Chekhov's bow. His world renown as a dramatist is based on a comparatively small body of work compared with his fictional output. His current reputation as a dramatist, rather than as a writer of short stories, would undoubtedly have come as a surprise to him. Indeed, up until six years before his death, he would probably have been reconciled to his fate as a failed dramatist, given his experience of the theatre and the attempts made to stage his plays during his lifetime. The one-act 'jokes', which he claimed to have written in hours rather than days, were produced just as successfully, if not more so, as the full-length plays which cost him so much time and effort, although the influence of the former on the latter should not be underestimated.

Staging of Chekhov's plays during his lifetime

The first production of *Ivanov*, at the Korsh Theatre, Moscow, in 1887 was under-rehearsed and something of a shambles, as Chekhov's letter to his brother testifies (Karlinsky and Heim, pp. 72–3). The revised version was subsequently staged in St Petersburg with greater success, but the première of *The Wood Demon*, at the Abramova Theatre, Moscow, in 1889 was as discouraging as the première of *Ivanov* had been. The first performance for *The Seagull* in 1896, which Chekhov attended in St Petersburg, was not so disastrous a production as history has suggested, largely because the director, Yevtikhy Karpov, was a highly competent producer and Vera Komissarzhevskaya, who played Nina, a very fine actress. The première was a flop largely because the audience had expected the première to be a benefit performance for one of the theatre's leading ladies and had arrived anticipating the typical comedy with which her reputation had been made. Not surprisingly, they were bitterly disappointed by the non-appearance of their favourite and totally bemused by the play, which called itself a 'comedy' and ended with a suicide.

Chekhov's dramatic rehabilitation was directly attributable to the enthusiastic propagandising of his merits by Vladimir Nemirovich-Danchenko, who was himself a dramatist and closely associated with the Maly Theatre, as well as being a teacher of drama and theatre studies at the Moscow Philharmonic School.

When deciding, together with Stanislavsky, on the repertoire for the Moscow Art Theatre's first season, it was Nemirovich who advocated reviving *The Seagull* in the face of his partner's general coolness towards the modern repertoire and ignorance of Chekhov's work. Chekhov needed some persuading in the wake of the 1896 débâcle but, reluctantly, agreed without any great hopes of success, given an untried company in untried circumstances. The rest is history. Stanislavsky prepared a detailed production score for the play (itself a very unusual procedure at the time – see S. D. Balukhaty (ed.), '*The Seagull*' *Produced by Stanislavsky*, 1952); the play then went into extended rehearsal and opened to great public acclaim in December 1898. Critics were rather less enthusiastic than the general public, however, and tended to dislike what they saw as the play's pessimism and the excessively naturalistic elements in its production. Chekhov was himself critical of the production when he was given a private performance, without décor, in 1899. He was especially critical of Stanislavsky's interpretation of Trigorin as a rather wan and spineless aesthete, as well as the interpretation of Nina as someone permanently overwrought.

The upshot was that, when trying to find an outlet for *Uncle Vanya* (his re-drafted version of *The Wood Demon*), Chekhov offered the play to the Maly Theatre. It was only because they required further rewriting that Chekhov withdrew his offer and handed the play to the Art Theatre instead. The première, given during the second season in 1899–1900 was, if anything, a greater success than that of *The Seagull*, despite the odd critical quibble. Gorky was overwhelmed by the experience of both reading the play and seeing it in performance. From this point on, Chekhov drew ever closer to the Art Theatre, largely on account of his attachment to the Theatre's leading lady, Olga Knipper. His last two plays were written especially for the Moscow Art Theatre and with specific members of the company in mind.

Three Sisters was given its première in January 1901 and, although not an instant success, confirmed Chekhov's status as a major dramatist. (For an account of the production based on Stanislavsky's score, see R. Russell and A. Barratt (eds.), *Russian Theatre in the Age of Modernism*, 1990.) Despite its description as a 'drama' on the play's title page, Chekhov insisted he had written 'a comedy'. Disputes about the generic nature of the work accompanied it at the time and have continued to do so ever since. Chekhov attended rehearsals and was particularly anxious about the accuracy of 'effects', such as that of the fire in Act Three. He also submitted to demands that the ending of the play be rewritten. In the original version, the body of the dead Baron was to be carried on stage but, fearing that the cramped conditions at the 'Ermitazh' theatre would not permit this without rocking the scenery, Stanislavsky asked that the scene be omitted. He also felt that the presence of the corpse rendered the play's ending too morbid – a point with which Chekhov concurred.

Stanislavsky's production of *The Cherry Orchard*

By the time the Moscow Art Theatre came to stage *The Cherry Orchard* in 1904, it had moved from the Ermitazh on Carriage Row to newly converted premises near the city centre (where it remains housed to this day). Chekhov was already terminally ill and the length of time he took to compose the play was due to the intense physical difficulties he was experiencing, quite apart from the intrinsic problems of writing the play. In the circumstances, it is amazing that what emerged was described by Chekhov as 'a comedy . . . even, in places, a farce'. Needless to say, Stanislavsky insisted that Chekhov did not understand what he had written and that the play was, by any normal standards, 'a tragedy'. He had been moved to tears whilst reading it. Despite Chekhov's protests, Stanislavsky began work on the production score firmly convinced that he was right and that the author was wrong. However, the actual score that emerged would seem to have been more faithful to Chekhov's intentions than has, hitherto, been assumed.

Despite his illness, Chekhov insisted on attending rehearsals. He sat at the back of the auditorium, refusing invitations to sit in the director's chair. He offered suggestions and comments, particularly on how best to achieve certain effects like the famous sound of the 'breaking string', all of which went unheeded. Eventually, he became disillusioned and stopped attending. Not only were his suggestions being ignored but almost every proposal he made with regard to casting was disregarded. He was especially anxious about the casting of Charlotta, whom he thought Knipper should have played. Knipper was less than suitably cast as Ranyevskaya and Charlotta's role was given to an actress whom Chekhov considered to lack a sense of humour. Chekhov had cast Stanislavsky as Lopakhin whilst composing the play, with the result that the Theatre chose Leonidov for the part. Stanislavsky played Gayev. And so on . . . Chekhov was both irritated by this and dismayed by reports he received during rehearsals, which seemed to give misleading accounts of the play's action. He concluded, after the première, that Stanislavsky had 'ruined' his play. Matters were not helped by his having been asked to cut the ending to Act Two and include some of its elements at the beginning of the act. When Chekhov died in July, approximately five months after the play's opening, he must have thought he would go down in history as a dramatist destined for the lower divisions of theatre history. However, to adapt Olga's final line in *Three Sisters*: If only he knew. If only he knew . . . !

It is difficult to find any evidence in Stanislavsky's production score that he considered *The Cherry Orchard* anything other than a comedy. Despite the production's reputation for 'heaviness', the actual score manifests an imaginativeness and lightness of touch, a grasp of certain 'vaudeville' elements in the play in a manner quite unlike the production score for *Three Sisters*. The score for *The Cherry Orchard* suggests that Stanislavsky had readily acquiesced in Chekhov's insistence that what he had written was, at times, 'a farce'. A contemporary critic, Alexander Kugel, normally hostile to the Art Theatre's naturalistic approach, thought that the production contained elements of the Russian *balagan* or fairground show. The wonder is that the production ever acquired a reputation for tragic solemnity and tearfulness in the first place. On the other hand, years later, when writing to another contemporary critic and Art Theatre enthusiast, Nikolay Efros, Nemirovich was still referring to the 'heaviness' of the Art Theatre's original approach to staging *The Cherry Orchard*, something which the characteristic features of the production score would seem to belie.

Meyerhold who read the play as a symbolist, 'Maeterlinckean' drama, expressed his feelings in a letter to Chekhov in 1904 (see *Meyerhold on Theatre, op. cit.*, pp. 33–4) and inveighed against the Arts Theatre's heavy handling of Act Three (in particular), which he thought should last about twenty minutes and which took three times as long in performance, largely because of Stanislavsky's extended treatment of the conjuring and disappearing tricks (on which the score lavishes pages of descriptive detail). In the published edition of the score, the first act alone consists of 189 notes covering twenty-two pages; the second act takes up eighteen pages and 179 director's notes while the third act consists of 229 notes spread over thirty-three pages and introduces a host of characters whom Chekhov does not call for. The final act (of which the last page is frustratingly missing) takes up sixteen pages of 111 notes, making a grand total of eighty-nine pages and 708 individual notes. (*Rezhisserskiye ekzemplyary K.S. Stanislavskogo*, 6 vols. 1898–1930, Vol. 3 (1901–1904) ed. I. N. Solov'eva, 1983, pp. 293–462.)

Stanislavsky's score for each act begins with an attempt to establish a sense of 'mood'. At the beginning of Act One, the shutters are closed, except in Anya's room which Stanislavsky, in a letter to Chekhov, suggested he wanted to associate with her – 'bright and virginal'. The upper, oval sections of the windows are open admitting a weak morning light. There is a glow of red light from the stove and the sound of creaking floorboards. Stanislavsky also specifies that he wants plaster flaking off the ceiling throughout and especially in Act Three during the dancing scenes. There is a guttering candle on stage, and off stage the howl of dogs, of which 'there are many on the estate'. A train whistle is heard and the distant sounds of a departing train followed by the noise of Lopakhin waking in an adjoining room. Dunyasha is asleep in the nursery. Lopakhin enters, dishevelled, yawning, stretching, shuddering, etc., before waking Dunyasha. Stanislavsky notes that a mousetrap stands in a corner and adds: 'In old houses this is a necessary possession.'

The extent to which mood is dependent on sound and lighting effects is apparent from this short extract and is a feature of Art Theatre productions for which Stanislavsky had already acquired a considerable reputation. Realising this, and fearful of excess, Chekhov stressed in a letter to Stanislavsky that the time of the year in Act Two was high summer when croaking frogs and other creatures were conspicuously absent. Despite some of Chekhov's legitimate misgivings, which extended to Stanislavsky's desire to convey the impression of a passing train, some of the act's key moments are effectively handled, such as the one preceding the entry of the passer-by which introduces the sound of the 'breaking string' for the first time.

This section of Act Two (p. 33) opens with '. . . a scene with mosquitoes'. (Ranyevskaya's line 'There goes Yepikhodov . . .' is absent from the production score as it was from Chekhov's original text; he added it later when revising the play for publication.) The score continues: 'Silence reigns, only a bird cries. The mosquitoes conquer; a new flock has arrived.' All sit sunk in thought swatting mosquitoes. Yasha and Dunyasha indulge in a flirtatious game in which each swats the other's insects. (Stanislavsky was very fond of 'mosquito' scenes as is evident from Act One of Uncle Vanya, in which he acted Astrov with a knotted handkerchief on his head as protection against them.) Gayev's address to the setting sun is delivered lying full-length in a hay stook, gesticulating towards the heavens. When reprimanded, he rapidly puts his hands over his mouth, covers his face with his hat and lies back with arms folded. Firs, tired of standing, rests on a gravestone and mutters. (Chekhov had insisted there were no gravestones and that this was simply a wayside shrine, not a neglected cemetery.) Stanislavsky then suggests that the sound which all hear, like the sound of a breaking string, be achieved thus: 'Extend three wires from the flies and attach to the floor of the stage (obviously the sound will depend on the metal of which the wires are made), one thick one (the density of the sound will depend on the thickness), one a little thinner, and a third which is thinner still (possibly made of different metals). Run a thick piece of rope across the strings. The first sound is the falling of the bucket. The other two an echo – that is, the sound wandering over the steppe. As accompaniment, or conclusion to this gamut of sounds – a light tremolo on a bass drum (thunder).' As late as the 1930s, Nemirovich was bewailing the fact that the Theatre had still not managed to come up with the right sound.

Stanislavsky's score for the end of Act Two is for the original version of the play, in which the two 'eccentrics', Charlotta and Firs, are left on stage together (see pp. lvii–lviii). There are valid arguments for the reinstatement of the original version of Act Two, although the present translator disagrees with them. Following the exit of Anya and Trofimov there is a pause, followed by a crackle of twigs, and Charlotta's entrance 'singing an absurd German song', which Stanislavsky suggests should be a nonsense song: '*Ein Seltserwasser – ohne, ein Seltserwasser mit, das macht zwei Seltserwasser mit ohne und mit mit – mit, mit, mit, mit. Zuke, puke, muke, muke, mit, mit, mit*', etc. Charlotta emerges stage-right and performs a somersault in the hay. In the distance Firs can be heard coming along the road. He is striking matches to light his way in the encircling gloom. Earlier, Stanislavsky has suggested that, whenever he is walking about outside, Firs is in the habit of wearing huge metal-rimmed spectacles to prevent his tripping over tree roots, etc. The corncrakes and frogs start up. 'Towards the end of the act the concert strengthens' (here Stanislavsky is clearly choosing to ignore Chekhov's hint). Firs, muttering, looks for something on the ground near the bench (something which Ranyevskaya has mislaid). He lights a match. Stanislavsky notes that Charlotta's business with the cucumber (p. lviii) probably won't be visible in the gloom. The episode with the cap (p. lvii) is turned into a ventriloquist's act. Charlotta speaks the German numbers 'with her stomach'. Firs' story about the murder is accompanied by Charlotta's lighting matches and placing them in her mouth. The red glow is matched by the red tail light of a passing train. The final directions for the scene (after Chekhov's own) run: 'Charlotta emits a noise which sounds like a cross between a cat, a cockerel and a pig, then repeats: "Twitch-twitch".' On the reverse side of the last page of the score for Act Two, which is dated 18 November 1903, Stanislavsky notes: 'Yepikhodov has broken whatever it is Lyubov Andreyevna has mislaid.'

A spirit of comic grotesquerie akin to Chekhov's one-act play *The Wedding* appears to have been given full rein in the conceptual realisation of Act Three. On paper, the production score is second cousin to Chekhov the writer of theatrical 'jokes'. Stanislavsky sets the scene for a 'totally unsuccessful ball'. There are not many people – the station-master and a postal clerk, a soldier in the serge uniform of the 'other ranks', a shop assistant in a jacket and red tie, a young boy dancing with the tall, thin daughter of the priest's wife. Stanislavsky lists a whole range of extras, thirteen of whom are included in the scene. Entered in the list, but then crossed out for some reason, are 'a mournful Jew and his simple, jewel-bedecked wife, together with their pale, intelligent son and his beautiful wife who sniffs smelling salts'. Among those included in the scene are Pishchik's daughter (an offstage presence in the play), a hairdresser, a billiard-playing German with a goatee beard, a village schoolteacher and his wife (a midwife), the owner of a flour mill, a fat landowner and his thin wife, and her four daughters, all in identical dresses, with whom no one wants to dance and who, in consequence, are forced to dance with each other. The daughters are described as constantly bringing their mother fruit and nuts from the tables, while she combs the hair of each with the same comb after every dance. There is also a telegraphist (similar to Yat in *The Wedding*) who comports himself in military style, has long moustaches, and wears a stiff shirt front which keeps popping out each time he dances. The food provided is of a very homespun order – fresh fruit, nuts and seltzer water, the last of which has been drunk but has not been replenished. This allows for a 'running gag' whereby people are constantly up-ending bottles in search of the dregs of something to drink.

The production ran for four hours with three intervals, starting at 8.00 p.m. and ending around midnight. Settings, as with all the Art Theatre productions of Chekhov, were by Victor Simov. After abandoning rehearsals, Chekhov appeared at the theatre on opening night despite being very ill. He arrived during the performance and came out on stage at the end of Act Three to listen to speeches in his honour, through which he was barely able to stand. He then stayed on and saw Act Four through to the end. On the day after the première he wrote in a letter to a friend: 'My play was put on yesterday, for which reason I'm in a bad mood' (Letter to I. L. Leontyev, 18 January 1904). The poet, K. D. Balmont, who was to translate some Maeterlinck plays for the Art Theatre, was said by Knipper to be wild about the production. She also reported that the famous Maly Theatre actress, Mariya Yermolova, who saw it on 15 March, had been moved to tears and had 'applauded warmly' (Letter of 16 March 1904). The first night audience had not been especially enthusiastic and the performances given in St Petersburg less than a month later were greeted with greater acclaim than in Moscow. After seeing the revised text through the press, Chekhov left for the German spa town of Badenweiler where he died on 2 July 1904.

Critical approaches to *The Cherry Orchard*

The history of the play's interpretation on the stage and on the page has been characterised by controversy. As we have seen, Chekhov was unable to agree with Stanislavsky on matters of staging. Gorky disliked the play on political grounds as it seemed to him to deal with socially worthless people. Most contemporary reviewers assumed that the play dealt with recognisable human beings in recognisable circumstances. Others, like Meyerhold, Kugel and Bely, viewed the play in more abstract, non-human terms as a metaphorical 'dance of death' performed by animated puppets (see pp. xix and xxiii). Generally speaking, these polar oppositions between the 'real' and the 'unreal', the 'humanist' and the 'Symbolist', have characterised criticism of the play ever since. The burden of criticism in the Soviet Union was, inevitably, weighted on the sociological and realistic side; that in the West has tended to emphasise the more 'Symbolist' aspects of the play – at least in literary critical terms; in terms of actual stage production, conventionally realistic interpretations may be said to have dominated both the Soviet and non-Soviet stages.

The other bone of contention concerns the generic status of the play as either comedy or tragedy. In a famous essay the distinguished American critic, Francis Fergusson, interpreted the play in the light of the work of the Ancient Greek dramatist, Sophocles, and Aristotle's *Poetics*, which have dominated Western thought about tragedy for the past two thousand years. He also drew comparisons with the work of the Italian Renaissance poet, Dante, one section of whose poem, *The Inferno*, is called 'The Valley of Negligent Rulers' – a fact which struck Fergusson as having connections with the negligence exhibited by the Russian landowning class in *The Cherry Orchard* (*The Idea of a Theatre*, 1949, pp. 174–90). The editor of a recent volume of essays has continued the classical analogy by referring to the sound of the breaking string as 'reminiscent of the final snipping of the thread by Atropos', one of the three Greek Goddesses of Fate, who cuts the Thread of Life which has been spun and wound by the other two. The same critic also described the play as 'a drama of death', in which 'people are made to act like melancholy puppets on a

string, dancing ritually as if in a state of benumbed dream'
(Barricelli, pp. 111–28).

Another distinguished American critic places more stress on the
importance of contemporary historical and social factors in
understanding the play. In a manner reminiscent of Strindberg's
preface to *Miss Julie* of 1888, he describes the inhabitants of the
estate as 'vestiges of the past which must be cleared away before
the future can take its proper form'. The orchard and this social
group 'are both ripe for the axe'. At the same time, in terms of
genre, he characterises the work as a 'blend of the heroic and the
absurd' as well as 'a tragic play composed almost entirely of comic
scenes'. As part of an attempt to characterise the co-existence of
the tragic and the comic, he coins the potent expression 'cosmic
vaudeville', implying a combination of 'universal' significance with
the play's echoes of circus clowning and music-hall entertainment
(Valency, pp. 251–88).

Harvey Pitcher is a notable defender of optimistic and 'humanist'
readings of Chekhov and will have no truck with either 'absurdists'
or with those 'realists' of the political school of Chekhov criticism,
such as the Soviet critic Yermilov, who go so far as to identify
someone like Anya as a potential revolutionary (*The Chekhov
Play*, 1973, pp. 158–212). Beverly Hahn, in addition to providing
a useful synopsis of differing approaches to the play, sees Chekhov
as defining a process of cultural transition from a feudal past to an
industrial, commercialised present. The sale of the cherry orchard
becomes associated with the loss of 'an ideal of rustic goodness'
accentuated by the encroachment of the industrial world in the
shape of the railway and the large town visible on the horizon in
Act Two. In defence of her argument, Hahn cites examples from
other plays and related art forms, adducing Shakespeare's *The
Winter's Tale* and the paintings of Jean Watteau (1684–1721),
whose landscapes have a fleeting and melancholy sense of the
transitoriness of life and human pleasures. She also interprets the
sound of the breaking string as 'the sound of social transition'.
Where she departs from conventional 'humanist' readings is in
attributing 'sinister significance' to the 'distasteful' Pishchik and
Yasha, and in characterising Charlotta's conjuring as 'an act of
psychic violence' directed against her employers (*Chekhov: A Study
of the Major Stories and Plays*, 1977, pp. 12–36).

Donald Rayfield, apparently influenced by early-twentieth-century Symbolist readings of the play, takes the more controversial aspects of Hahn's reading even further. For this prominent English Chekhovian, humanity is 'dead' in *The Cherry Orchard* and the characters are 'ghosts'. They are also described as 'subhuman in their grotesquerie', in a play where only the trees in the cherry orchard are alive and where nature is the only possible tragic hero. (This opposition between human and natural worlds is commonly seen as a characteristic feature of Chekhov's drama.) More controversially, the critic finds Yepikhodov's obtuse and pretentious manner of speaking to contain thinly disguised obscenities, and characterises him as a 'spirit of evil' who walks 'to and fro across the stage' like Satan. (This refers to the moment in Act Two where he crosses the stage strumming his guitar.) Pishchik and Charlotta are described as mere 'flotsam in the wreckage of the estate'. (*Chekhov: The Evolution of his Art*, 1975, pp. 220–7).

In a review of Russian approaches to Chekhov the dramatist, Victor Terras describes the Symbolist writer and theorist, Dmitri Merezhkovsky, as 'likening life as shown in Chekhov's last plays . . . to a condition of non-being, or the existence of the living dead' (*The Chekhov Companion*, p. 169) – a view which would seem to lend support to Donald Rayfield's. One of the most prominent critical approaches to emerge from Terras's survey is that of the Russian Formalists, who were active during the 1920s, and who tended to look at literary works ahistorically and in terms of their formal, linguistic and structural features. They valued a work of art to the extent that its formal features 'defamiliarised' our perception of the world, rendering it strange and, therefore, causing us to perceive it with the freshness of unfamiliarity. Their method even extended to the tabulation of dramatic pauses. For example, the doyen of Russian Formalist Chekhov critics, S. D. Balukhaty, calculated that *The Cherry Orchard* contained ten pauses in Act One, seventeen in Act Two, only one in Act Three and fifteen in Act Four. Whilst agreeing with others that the action is developed 'in the unique style of the grotesque' (from the Italian *grottesco* describing comically distorted or exaggerated figures), he characterised this process in purely formal terms, as one based on a style of dramatic composition in which linguistic *devices* (a key

Formalist concept) of interruption, or repetition, stand out (Robert L. Jackson ed., pp. 136–46).

One of the best-known characterisations of Chekhov's method has been that of the critic and translator, David Magarshack, in one of the first, and therefore highly influential, English studies of Chekhov's plays. In this, he referred to early works such as *Platonov* and *Ivanov* as plays of 'direct action' and later plays, such as *The Seagull, Uncle Vanya, Three Sisters* and *The Cherry Orchard*, as plays of 'indirect action'. In the former 'the main dramatic action takes place on the stage in full view of the audience'; in the latter 'the main dramatic action takes place off stage' and that which does take place in view of the audience is mainly 'inner action' (*Chekhov the Dramatist*, 1952, p. 53). In this latter sense, characters are seen to be subject to an invisible process which could be attributable, naturalistically, to the determining pressures of the past or it could be defined, in more abstract terms as 'the suffering of change' (Francis Fergusson, *op. cit.*) or even the unseen, corrosive action of Time itself.

The theme of 'Time' has been noted by critics as an important feature of Chekhov's plays, including *The Cherry Orchard*, where past and present seem to merge and characters are constantly recalling the past or anticipating the future. The theme of childhood is prominent throughout. A critic very conscious of this is Valentine Bill, who singles out the number of occasions on which years, months, weeks, days, minutes and dates are referred to in *The Cherry Orchard* as well as pointing to the recurrence of phrases such as 'What time is it?' 'It's time to go', 'There isn't much time to talk', 'There's no time to lose', etc. There are also very precise references in the play to clock time: 'four o'clock', 'half-past nine', 'forty-six minutes', 'twenty minutes', etc. as well as to age and the ageing process (Valentine Tschebotarioff Bill, *Chekhov: The Silent Voice of Freedom*, 1987, pp. 123–4). As Bill suggests: 'It is time itself that all three characters most intimately connected with the estate are vainly attempting to escape, to deny, to arrest, to stop its destructive advance' (p. 234).

For Laurence Senelick, the time motif in the play contains an 'awareness that reality stands outside time', and he compares this aspect of the play with the work of Maurice Maeterlinck. In Act

Two, the characters seem to '. . . meet on a road halfway between past and present . . . being and nothingness'. There is much to be said in support of this 'Beckettian' reading, in the sense that the world of *The Cherry Orchard* is full of people who are just versions of wayfarers through life or respectable varieties of tramp (as in Samuel Beckett's *Waiting for Godot*, 1953). The 'now you see them, now you don't' aspect of the play is also apparent in moments such as Yepikhodov's passage over the stage in Act Two: 'There goes Yepikhodov . . .', in the constant coming and going of the characters, and in the disappearing tricks of Act Three. Senelick also points to the multitude of offstage presences – the 'invisible beings' who fortify 'the sense of the estate's vulnerability, transience and isolation'. He also, rather chillingly, mentions the 'cortège' of the offstage dead who include Ranyevskaya's husband, child, mother, and many others. Among those Senelick does not mention are Charlotta's parents. Appropriately enough, it is the child who used to perform the *salto mortale* (the death-defying leap) who has survived the ravages of time and who, orphaned, appears in a state of comic philosophical anxiety, speculating on her reasons for living. According to Logan Speirs, Charlotta 'haunts the play like a comic skeleton at a feast' (*Tolstoy and Chekhov*, 1971, p. 219), whilst Senelick concludes that 'Gogol, rather than Turgenev, is the presiding genius of the comedy' (*Anton Chekhov*, 1985, pp. 117–34).

In the Introduction to his translation, Michael Frayn insists we now know that 'Chekhov's characters are never puppets' (p. l). Nevertheless, a good deal of Chekhov criticism seems to assume that, to some extent, they are. Even Harvey Pitcher points to the use of the term *nyeskladny*, meaning 'disjointed', and speaks of a 'set of characters' who 'refuse to be quite fitted together' (Pitcher, *op. cit.*, p. 190). If they are to be construed in this way, to what extent ought this to be presented in naturalistic terms as an extension of their 'determined' nature and a consequence of genetic inheritance and environmental conditioning? Or should the presentation be more abstract and 'metaphysical'? Can human significance be reduced to a simplified pattern of arm-waving (Lopakhin), billiard strokes and sweet-sucking (Gayev), spilled money, dropped telegrams, even mislaid children (Ranyevskaya), broken or crushed objects (Yepikhodov), rhetorical flourishes and mislaid galoshes (Trofimov), senseless muttering (Firs), cucumber chewing, conjuring tricks and nut-eating dogs (Charlotta) . . . etc.?

At a more practical level, the play itself raises a number of unanswered questions in addition to the one as to how it is that Varya has come to be adopted (see p. xlvii). For example, how is it that Lopakhin has made a 40,000 rouble profit from 3,000 acres of poppies? What happens to Anya at the end of the play? Do she and Trofimov in fact 'join their lives to work for the future good of mankind' as Laurence Senelick suggests (*op. cit.*, p. 118), or does she stay with her uncle? Why, whenever Pishchik sends regards from 'Dashenka', does nobody ever reciprocate or, indeed, make any response whatever, let alone acknowledge her existence? At a more complicated level, is there any significance to be attached to notions of sleep, dream, daze and blows to the head which recur throughout? Is there a sense in which to be 'tied' is preferable to being freed, remembering that Firs considers emancipation to have been a 'disaster'? If so, does this affect an interpretation of the meaning of the breaking string? Is it apparent, as Siegfried Melchinger suggests and as Trevor Griffiths implies in the preface to his own version of the play (London, 1978), that 'at the time when *The Cherry Orchard* was written, the years before the revolution of 1905, he [Chekhov] considered revolution in Russia irreversible and desirable' (Melchinger, *Anton Chekhov*, 1972, p. 148)? How valid is it to root the play in the specificity of social and historical conditions, 'lending an ear . . . to impending change' in the manner of 'other works stemming from the period of hush before the First World War' (Fergusson, p. 157)? Finally, why does Chekhov ask in this play for that which he does not ask in any of his other plays, namely, that at certain points in the action the stage should be 'empty'?

Production history

Russian productions
Despite the popularity of Chekhov's plays, *The Cherry Orchard* has not been staged very frequently in his homeland. This is largely because, after the Revolution, Soviet artistic policy tended to identify the mood of Chekhov's drama with a pre-revolutionary world and its negative ambience. There have been no major

revivals at the Moscow Art Theatre since the original 1904
production, the version which was brought to London in 1958
being essentially the same 1904 version, but as revised in 1929. A
recent Art Theatre production by Oleg Yefremov, which sought to
parody the plight of the estate's inhabitants, was not particularly
successful. Some of its effects included an attempt to suggest the
characters' second childhood by recreating an actual nursery
complete with rocking-horse, behind a scrim at the rear of the
stage which, as in a pantomime, could be seen through when lit
from behind, revealing Ranyevskaya at one point, astride the horse.
The attempt to convey the feeling of a bygone epoch dependent on
an underclass was suggested by having a statically servile Firs,
patiently withstanding bombardment between the acts from a snow
cannon – a device seemingly designed to bury him in an everlasting
drift. The production also featured 'the Russian Hamlet', Innokenti
Smoktunovsky, as Gayev, in one of his last performances before his
death.

The Leningrad Theatre of Comedy staged the play as a satire in
1924 and ten years later, Reuben Simonov's Studio attached to the
Vakhtangov Theatre attempted an experimental production in
which the degeneracy of the pre-revolutionary gentry was conveyed
by hinting at an affair between Ranyevskaya and Yasha and by
turning Lopakhin, whom Chekhov emphasised was a thoroughly
decent individual, into a money-grubbing *kulak*. An attempt was
made in Nizhny-Novgorod in 1929 to stage the play as a farce, but
probably the most notable Russian revival this century has been
that staged at the Moscow Taganka Theatre in 1975, directed by
Anatoli Efros. The production starred Vladimir Vysotsky, a
Russian James-Dean-cum-Bob-Dylan who had recently acted
Hamlet, and who portrayed a rather unorthodox Lopakhin
opposite Alla Demidova's neurotic, fashion-conscious
Ranyevskaya. The stylised setting combined external elements of a
graveyard with internal features such as billowing curtains and
family portraits. In 1994, the Maly Drama Theatre, from St
Petersburg, brought their recent production of the play, directed by
Lev Dodin, to the Lyric Theatre, Hammersmith, as part of the
company's British tour, where it was performed in Russian with
sur-titles. It was a very tactile production, in which characters were
constantly in physical contact with each other, communicating a

sense of 'adolescent recklessness' (*Guardian*). The set consisted of a 'narcissistic forest of tall-framed and dusty windows-cum-mirrors' (*Independent*) and included moments of pure slapstick, such as the one when Yepikhodov toppled head-first into a pond to re-emerge soaking wet and clutching a flat-iron, while Dunyasha and Yasha stole a kiss behind his back. One of the most interesting aspects of the production was its decision to restore the original ending of Act Two.

Other non-British productions

One of the most famous non-British productions has probably been Peter Brook's French version, staged with an international cast in Paris in 1981, and later staged in English, in New York in 1988, and in Moscow in 1989 with a changed cast. The production exploited an open stage with few items of furniture – one or two screens and a bookcase – and with oriental rugs covering the stage floor. Where Peter Brook's productions are normally characterised by strong ensemble work, this one tended to suffer from the fact that its personnel were constantly changing. Michel Piccoli in Paris, Brian Dennehy in New York and Tom Wilkinson in Moscow all acted very different versions of Lopakhin. Rebecca Miller, daughter of the American dramatist Arthur Miller, played Anya both in New York and in Moscow. The only permanent members of the cast appear to have been Peter Brook's wife, Natasha Parry, who played Ranyevskaya, and Erland Josephson (of Ingmar Bergman film fame) who played Gayev. One of the most successful moments of a production, which in many ways was among the least typical of Brook's work, was the third act dance, when to the skittering, high-pitched rhythms of a Jewish orchestra the dancers flitted rapidly across the rear of the stage, each performing a comic *entrechat* when passing the doorway.

Nemirovich-Danchenko was responsible for a production in Milan in 1933 (as guest director, and with the emigrée actress Tatyana Pavlova as Ranyevskaya), in which he attempted to bring out some of the play's comic elements. The film director, Luchino Visconti, directed the play in Rome in 1966, but probably the most significant Italian production was that staged by Giorgio Strehler at his Piccolo Teatro, Milan, in 1955. The theme of a return to childhood was its leitmotiv, from the child's tea-service and school desks on stage in Act One to the toy train which chugged around the stage in Act Two. Intense white light lent the production an incandescent quality in which the sound of the breaking string was achieved in complete silence accompanied by the sudden tremulous billowing of a veil hung over the entire stage. Elsewhere on the continent, Jean-Louis Barrault's 1954 Paris production at the Théâtre Marigny aimed for a sense of 'mood' rather than everyday realism and attempted to slow down the pace of a play which, in French, tended to be played so rapidly that a great deal of the sub-text went for nothing.

The play does not appear to have been very popular in Germany. First staged in 1919, it was revived by Peter Zadek in 1968 and again by Rudolph Noelte in 1970. In 1988, Peter Stein staged a production at the Berlin Schaubühne which Michael Billington, the *Guardian* theatre critic, described as 'simply, the best Chekhov production I have ever encountered'. This was in the wake of the same director's version of *Three Sisters*, which was given an enthusiastic reception when shown in Moscow. Stein's answer to the problems which the play poses was to push its disparate elements – tragedy, comedy, pastoral, farce – to the very limit. As Billington remarked: 'In this version the realism is more realistic, the symbolism more symbolic and the farce funnier than in any of the dozen other productions I have seen.' The production had a sense 'of life lived at fever pitch, touching the wildest extremities of absurdity and pain'. The sound of the breaking string was accompanied by the sudden illumination of the backcloth with a distant prospect of industrial chimneys and Kremlin domes 'implying the Revolution to come'. At the moment of Firs' 'death' in the abandoned house, a lopped branch crashed 'suddenly and terrifyingly' through the shuttered window shattering the glass to smithereens.

America has had its fair share of *Cherry Orchard* productions, in which many of the pioneering efforts were those of emigrés. Alla Nazimova, who began her career at the Moscow Art Theatre, starred in a production of *The Cherry Orchard* at the Civic Repertory Theatre in 1928 and 1933, directed by a stalwart of American Chekhov, Eve le Gallienne, who revived the play again in 1944, when she acted Ranyevskaya herself. Joshua Logan wrote and directed his own version of the play as *The Wisteria Trees*, at the Martin Beck Theatre, New York, in 1950, with the action removed to a post-Civil War Southern plantation. The servants on the estate were all black, former slaves and Lopakhin had made his money in cotton. This was followed, logically enough, by an all-black *Cherry Orchard* in 1973, in which the landowners were portrayed with lighter skins than the servants and the Act Two passer-by was an impoverished black South African who spoke in dialect. The Rumanian director, Andrei Serban, staged the play at the Beaumont Theatre, New York, in 1977, with a cast which combined the talents of experienced actors such as Irene Worth (Ranyevskaya) with those of up-and-coming Hollywood stars such as Meryl Streep (Dunyasha). Serban, from an Eastern European background, was seen to be attempting to exorcise the Stanislavskyan inheritance by emphasising the play's farcical elements and by filling the stage with visual metaphors. These included a cage-like balloon, a plough dragged across a field by peasants and, at the end, a cherry branch placed in front of an enormous factory (*Chekhov Companion*, p. 223).

British productions

As far as British productions of Chekhov and of this particular play are concerned, we are indebted to the work of Patrick Miles, both as author of *Chekhov on the British Stage 1909–1987* (1987) and as editor of *Chekhov on the British Stage* (1993). The former is a comprehensive reference list of British productions of Chekhov between the dates mentioned, presented in the form of extracts from reviews and linked by the author's commentary. The second volume consists of essays by divers hands, mainly Russian, British and American, and includes a selective chronology of British professional productions of Chekhov's plays 1909–1991. This credits twenty-seven productions of the play so far this century, including visiting versions given by the Prague Group of the Moscow Art Theatre in 1928 and 1931 and the Moscow Art Theatre in 1958.

The first professional production of *The Cherry Orchard* in English was on 28 May 1911 at the Aldwych Theatre, London. Other notable productions in the sequence which followed include John Gielgud's appearance as Trofimov in a production directed by J. B. Fagan at the Lyric Theatre, Hammersmith, in 1925, and Theodore Komissarzhevsky's 1926 production at the Barnes Theatre, London. The latter established an important link between Russian and English Chekhov productions. Komissarzhevsky had worked in the Russian Theatre before emigrating after the Revolution and knew of the Moscow Art Theatre's work at first hand. His sister, Vera, had starred in the 1896 première of *The Seagull* and his father had worked closely with Stanislavsky in the latter's pre-Art Theatre days. He was also married for a short time to Peggy Ashcroft, who became one of this country's finest interpreters of Chekhovian roles. Tyrone Guthrie's 1933 production at the Old Vic had a cast which included Charles Laughton (Lopakhin), Flora Robson (Varya) and Athene Seyler (Ranyevskaya). John Gielgud directed his own translation of the play at the Lyric Hammersmith in 1954 with Trevor Howard as Lopakhin and Gwen Ffrangcon-Davies as Ranyevskaya; and Michel Saint-Denis staged Gielgud's version again in 1961 at the Aldwych Theatre, with Peggy Ashcroft (Ranyevskaya), Gielgud himself as Gayev, Dorothy Tutin as Varya and Judi Dench as Anya. Peter Hall staged a production with an all-star cast at the National Theatre in 1978, memorable for its very expensive silkscreen backcloth to Act Two and Ralph Richardson's wonderfully understated performance as Firs, 'a masterly creation worthy of the Moscow Art at its Stanislavsky best', according to Sheridan Morley (*Shooting Stars*, London, 1983, pp. 119–21). It was for this production that the present version of the play was prepared. Describing Michael Frayn's translation as 'super-cool' and 'a model of non-commitment', the same critic accused the actual production of lacking a guiding thesis or theory, as well as social, historical or political comment. The actors portrayed 'overgrown children in some eternal nursery [. . .] adrift in a world where even the furniture seems no longer quite as friendly as it once was'.

Less mainstream, but also memorable for various reasons, were the two productions of Trevor Griffiths' 'political' version of the play, staged at the Nottingham Playhouse in 1977 and later shown on television, both directed by Richard Eyre, and Peter Gill's emotionally-charged production at the Riverside Studios, London,

1978, in which real tears were very much in evidence. The two attempts at staging the play made by Lindsay Anderson, in 1966 with Tom Courtney as Trofimov, and in 1983 with Joan Plowright as Ranyevskaya and Frank Finlay as Lopakhin, were neither of them very successful despite the director's obvious empathy with the play. The disappointment of the first attempt owed something to inadequate rehearsal and a clash of styles. The result was that the attempt to 'take a fresh look at a masterpiece' had a 'dullness' which 'left the play expiring on its feet' (Peter Roberts, *Plays and Players*, September, 1966). Anderson's second production was rather unkindly described as having a 'veneer of old-fashioned repertory company theatricality' with 'the glazed look of verisimilitude a few degrees removed from the living . . . like a painstakingly stuffed bird pinned to an Edwardian lady's hat' (Martin Hoyle, *Plays and Players*, December, 1983).

A production which does not feature in Patrick Miles's list, is the première of American playwright David Mamet's 'adaptation' of *The Cherry Orchard*, given in Harrogate in April 1989. The play, according to Mamet, is all about sex: 'Nobody in the play gives a damn about the cherry orchard . . . The play is a series of scenes about sexuality and, particularly, frustrated sexuality.' However, according to Robin Thornber in *The Guardian*, the fine production showed little evidence of Mamet's own theories, whilst the audience demonstrated its appreciation 'of being offered first class, world class theatre' by greeting the première performance with 'a tumult of applause'.

Problems of Chekhov translation

Laurence Senelick, who has made his own translation of *The Cherry Orchard*, provides a salutary reminder of the problems facing any would-be renderer of Chekhov into English. As he notes, each character is distinguished by an appropriate speech pattern. Ranyevskaya constantly employs diminutives and uses vague expressions; Gayev deploys a mixture of the fulsomely oratorical and the abruptly interrogative, e.g., '*Chego?*' ('Who?' in the present translation), which sounds 'more effete' than the more usual '*Chto?*' ('What?'). Pishchik speaks in breathless phrases which are 'a hodge-podge of old-world courtesy, hunting terms and newspaper talk'; Lopakhin's language is socially varied and depends on whom he is addressing; Trofimov's is a *mélange* of the poetic, the literary and the political, whereas Yepikhodov invents a style of 'educated' discourse which is all his own and which, as Dunyasha points out, does not make sense a lot of the time (Senelick, *op. cit.*, p. 133). Chekhov himself pointed out that Charlotta speaks good Russian (and therefore good English) without an accent but that 'sometimes she confuses masculine and feminine adjectival endings'. As English is not an inflected language like Russian, it becomes the translator's problem to convey a sense of this masculine/feminine confusion which is clearly an aspect of her own confused identity.

Another problem facing the translator concerns Chekhov's persistent use of ellipses both within and at the ends of sentences. How faithful should a translator be to this trait while rendering dialogue which remains actable, without too many (for the English-speaking actor) unnatural tailings-off, interruptions, pauses, etc. In this case, it is interesting to compare Elizaveta Fen's translation of *The Cherry Orchard*, which observes nearly all the ellipses, with the present one, which observes some, but not all of them, and Ronald Hingley's version which eliminates all of them, substituting a single dash in places. Take this extract from the beginning of Act Two (p. 24):

Chekhov:

DUNYASHA (*smushchenno*). Khorosho . . . tol'ko snachala prinesitye mnye moyu tal'mochku . . . Ona okolo shkapa . . . tut nyemnozhko syro . . .

YEPIKHODOV. Khorosho-s . . . prinesu-s . . . Teper' ya znayu, chto mnye delat' s moim revol'verom . . .

DUNYASHA (*embarrassed*). All right . . . only first fetch my cloak . . . You'll find it by the cupboard . . . it's rather damp here . . .

YEPIKHODOV. Very well, ma'am . . . I will, ma'am . . . Now I know what to do with my revolver . . .

Fen:

DOONIASHA (*embarrassed*). Very well then . . . only will you

bring me my little cape first. . . . It's hanging beside the
wardrobe. It's rather chilly here. . . .

YEPIKHODOV. Very well, I'll bring it. . . . Now I know what to
do with my revolver.

Frayn:

DUNYASHA (*embarrassed*). All right – only first fetch my cloak.
You'll find it by the cupboard. It's rather damp here.

YEPIKHODOV. Now I know what to do with my revolver . . .

Hingley:

DUNYASHA (*embarrassed*). Very well then, only first go and get
me my cape. You'll find it in the cupboard or somewhere. It's
rather damp out here.

YEPIKHODOV. Oh certainly, I'm sure. At your service. Now I
know what to do with my revolver.

At a more mundane level, does Lopakhin 'bleat' or 'moo' when he
interrupts the conversation between Anya and Varya in Act One?
Translators interpret the word *mychit* as both one and the other.
Whether the girls are to be seen as 'silly cows' or 'lambs to the
slaughter' might be a valid interpretative quibble. Another
question, relating to Lopakhin, concerns his rendering into English
of quotations from *Hamlet*. The Russian original is already, in a
sense, a 'misquotation'. But Lopakhin misquotes a misquotation as
well as getting Ophelia's name wrong and confusing a nunnery
with a monastery. Some translators, who believe Lopakhin gets
Shakespeare nearly right *in English*, have even been known to go
so far as to suggest that the play which Lopakhin refers to having
been at the previous night (in Act Two) was probably *Hamlet*!

One of the main bones of contention surrounds the translation
of the phrase used by Firs – *nyedotyopa* ('sillybilly' in the present
edition) – which Michael Frayn believes derives from the Ukrainian
dotepa, meaning a clever or witty person, and its opposite,
nedotepa. The actual word 'sillybilly', in English, refers to the
foolish partner in a double act and belongs to the tradition of
fairground performance. However, Ozhegov's *Dictionary of the
Russian Language* says that the word *nyedotyopa* is a colloquial/
metaphorical expression meaning 'an unintelligent person who is
inept and clumsy in every respect'. In a recent article by Valentina

Ryapolova, in which the Russian critic accords high praise to
Michael Frayn's translations of Chekhov (*Chekhov on the British
Stage*, pp. 226–36), she explains the etymology of the expression
and makes it plain that, in Russian (if Chekhov was thinking of the
Russian expression rather than the Ukrainian), the word refers to
something which has been hacked into a crude form but is
essentially unfinished; 'half-cut' would convey the wrong
associations in English, whereas 'rough-hewn' or 'half-finished'
achieve a better sense of the meaning, and might even be seen to
connect with the hewing down of the orchard. The analogy is with
a wooden image which has been fashioned very crudely. The term,
in this sense, contains within it a hint of Richard III's complaint
that he has been sent into the world 'deformed, unfinished . . .
scarce half made up', but it is difficult to find a precise English
equivalent for the Russian expression, as the plethora of variants
with each fresh translation of the play bears witness to.
Yepikhodov's nickname '*Dvadtsat' dva neschastya*' also provides
grist for the translator's mill. Meaning literally 'Twenty-two
misfortunes', the present translation's 'Disasters by the Dozen' is
one of the happier variants.

    There are other interpretative problems for which a translator
cannot be blamed directly. For example, an excessively zealous,
clue-hunting student who was interested in what she detected to be
'knockabout' and 'Punch and Judy' elements in the play, made
much of the blows to the head which Lopakhin refers to, or
receives. This was then connected with the 'club' which comes
down on Ranyevskaya's head (on p. 28) and the 'poker' with
which the numbers have been burned into the bookcase (on p. 12).
In fact, neither of these objects appears in the original text.
Brought into this translation, they are merely attempts to flesh out,
or to render more vivid, expressions in English which capture the
sense and flavour of the original.

    Another time-honoured problem concerns the rendering of the
Chekhovian stage direction *skvoz' slyozy* (meaning, literally,
'through tears'), especially since Chekhov declared that there was
only one 'cry-baby' in the play, Varya, and denied the existence of
any real tears throughout. As will be noted, if the interested
student chooses to compare Michael Frayn's 1978 translation with
the revised 1988 version, he also had problems with the

expression, indicated by his having had second thoughts. The decision to render the usual 'eternal' student as 'wandering' (for the reasons suggested on p. xlix) seems a brilliant stroke, in keeping with the feeling that everyone – from Varya the would-be pilgrim to the eternally restless Ranyevskaya – are varieties of 'wanderer through life'.

How important are fairly minor questions of translation? For instance, ought the diminutive of Leonid (Gayev) to be Lenya or Lyonya? It may seem a trivial matter but Richard Peace's study of Chekhov (*Chekhov: A Study of the Four Major Plays*, 1983) makes a point of the significant connection between the Russian word for laziness (*len'*) and Lenya, when other translators, as well as the editor of the authoritative Bradda edition of the play, cite 'Lyonya' as the diminutive form. Anyone interested in these finer points is advised to consult the relevant essays in *Chekhov on the British Stage*, as well as Eugene Bristow's examination of nine translations published between 1912 and 1985 referred to by Lauren G. Leighton in the *Chekhov Companion* (p. 303).

Further Reading

Jean-Pierre Barricelli (ed.), *Chekhov's Great Plays: A Critical Anthology* (New York University Press, 1981). Contains seventeen essays by divers hands on all the late plays (Part One), and on themes/motifs in Chekhov's plays as well as their early production history (Part Two).

Anton Chekhov, *Plays* (*The Seagull, Uncle Vanya, Three Sisters, The Cherry Orchard, The Evils of Tobacco, Swan Song, The Bear, The Proposal*), trans. and intro. by Michael Frayn (Methuen, London, 1988).

——, *The Complete Plays*, trans., ed., and annotated by Laurence Senelick (W.W. Norton & Co., New York/London, 2006).

Toby W. Clyman (ed.), *A Chekhov Companion* (Greenwood Press, Connecticut/London, 1985). Seventeen essays by divers hands arranged in seventeen sections and covering many different aspects of Chekhov's work and its reception.

Victor Emeljanov (ed.), *Chekhov: The Critical Heritage* (Routledge & Kegan Paul, London, 1981). Selections from early criticism of Chekhov's work and a selection of production reviews in America and Great Britain culled from newspapers and magazines between 1911 and 1945.

Ronald Hingley, *A New Life of Chekhov* (Oxford University Press, 1976). The standard biography by one of Chekhov's leading translators.

Robert Louis Jackson (ed.), *Chekhov: A Collection of Critical Essays* (Prentice Hall, New Jersey, 1967). A very useful anthology of fifteen essays, mostly on Chekhov the playwright, by an international group of critics which includes a number of Russians.

Simon Karlinsky (ed. and trans.) and Michael Henry Heim (trans.), *Letters of Anton Chekhov* (Bodley Head, London, 1973). A broad selection of letters with separate sections on individual plays and with extremely helpful and informative commentary.

Irina and Igor Levin, *Working on the Play and the Role: The Stanislavsky Method for Analyzing the Characters in a Drama* (Ivan R. Dee, Chicago, 1992). The bulk of this 186-page book is taken up with an analysis of how *The Cherry Orchard* might be staged using Stanislavsky's system of actor training.

Donald Rayfield, *The Cherry Orchard: Catastrophe and Comedy* (Twayne's Masterwork Series, G. K. Hall & Co., Boston, 1994). One of a well-established series of critical texts aimed at a student and undergraduate readership.

——, *Anton Chekhov: A Life* (Harper Collins, London, 1997). The most recent biographical study of Chekhov using post-Soviet archival material freed from former censorship restrictions.

John McKellor Reid, *The Polemical Force of Chekhov's Comedies: A Rhetorical Analysis* (Edwin Mellen Press, Lewiston/Queenston/ Lampeter, 2007). A recent study which combines an academic approach with a strong sense of stage performance.

Laurence Senelick, *The Chekhov Theatre: A Century of the Plays in Performance* (Cambridge University Press, 1997). An exhaustive study of the most significant productions of Chekhov's plays worldwide since 1904.

J.L. Styan, *Chekhov in Performance: A Commentary on the Major Plays* (Cambridge University Press, 1971). The only study of Chekhov's major plays which interprets each in terms of performance on a scene-by-scene basis.

Anton Tchekhov, *La Cerisaie* (The Cherry Orchard), with preface, commentary and notes by Patrice Pavis (Livre de Poche, Paris, 1988). Valuable editorial commentary and notes (in French) by one of the foremost contemporary theatrical theoreticians.

Maurice Valency, *The Breaking String: The Plays of Anton Chekhov* (Oxford University Press, 1966). Contains essays on most of the full-length plays, preceded by a very ample introduction to Chekhov's nineteenth-century theatrical background.

Nick Worrall, *File on Chekhov* (Methuen, London, 1986). One of the Methuen Writer-Files series and containing synopses of all Chekhov's plays, together with commentary culled from Chekhov's correspondence and selections from reviews of the plays in production.

——, 'Stanislavsky's Production Score for Chekhov's *The Cherry Orchard* (1904): A Synoptic Overview' in *Modern Drama*, vol. xlii, no. 4, winter 1999, pp. 519–40. Attempts to reconstruct the first production of *The Cherry Orchard* on the basis of Stanislavsky's prompt-book.

Translator's Introduction

By the time Chekhov came to write *The Cherry Orchard*, in 1903, he was dying. This final play gave him one of the hardest struggles he had ever had. His tuberculosis left him increasingly exhausted, while his waning strength was further eroded by the discomfort of his life in Yalta, and by travelling back and forth to Moscow because of disagreement between his doctors about which climate would suit him best. There was tension in the household, too, between his sister, Masha, and his new wife, Olga Knipper; while the short hours of his working day were wasted by the perpetual stream of visitors that his fame attracted. In the end the play was a triumph, and at the first performance, on 17 January 1904, his forty-fourth birthday, he was brought up on stage between acts three and four for lengthy speeches and presentations. But by this time he was visibly failing; he had only another four months to live.

It was the play itself that presented the greatest problems. He had been thinking about it for two years before he began to write, and it had been conceived from the very first as a comedy. 'The next play that I write,' he said in a letter to Knipper in March, 1901, 'will definitely be a funny one, a very funny one, at any rate in conception.' In another letter he described it as 'a four-act vaudeville,' and in the autumn of that year, according to Stanislavsky, he gave the actors at the Moscow Arts a kind of oral trailer for what he had in mind. Three of the four disconnected details he produced were essentially comic: a servant who went fishing; a cheerful billiards enthusiast with a loud voice and only one arm; and the owner (male or female) of a country estate who kept borrowing money off the servant. This list may have been more in the nature of a whimsical camouflage for his intentions than a serious exposition of them – it would have been very much his style. He may even have been joking when he included as the fourth item an even smaller and more disconnected detail: 'a branch of cherry blossom sticking out of the garden straight into the room through an open window.'

From this one tiny visual flourish, however, came the real play – and all his difficulties with accommodating it to his original comic conception. During the course of the next two years he must have traced that branch back out of the window – back to the orchard in which the tree was rooted, back to the social history and economic forces which explained why that orchard had been planted and why it was now about to be felled. The trail took him not only outwards through Russian society and across the Russian landscape, but backwards in time through his own writing and his own life. From where he now stood, on the brink of his last work, and at the end of his life, he found himself returning to themes he had touched upon in his stories over his entire professional career, and going back further still, to his childhood. As a schoolboy in Taganrog he had heard stories told by the mother of one of his friends about her life as a landowner before the Emancipation (on an estate where there was an ancient serf like Firs) in Poltava province, which was famous for its cherry orchards. He had spent summer holidays as a child on a rural estate out in the steppe to the north of Taganrog, where his grandfather (a manumitted serf himself) was steward. He had heard the distant sound of a breaking cable in the mines while he was staying with a boyhood friend on another property in the steppe. His own modest family home had been sold off to pay his father's debts – and bought by the wealthy friend who had promised to save it. By the time he began to write the play, that single branch at the window had led him to a world which was remarkably difficult to accommodate in a 'four-act vaudeville'.

In fact *The Cherry Orchard* is the most elusive and difficult of all these four last plays. There are not only the mysteries that all his other late plays contain. (Why has Ranyevskaya adopted Varya? There is no mention of her background or parentage. Is she known – to everyone but us – to be the illegitimate daughter of Ranyevskaya's drunken late husband?) The whole approach has become noticeably less naturalistic, and more dependent upon mood and symbolism. (Chekhov may have been planning to go further in this direction with the extraordinary new departure he was contemplating at the time of his death – a play about Arctic exploration.) It is also even less directly dramatic. The conflict from which the play springs is intense; the Gayev family is being broken apart by powerful forces – forces rooted deep in history and in the society around them. But in the whole course of the play only one dramatic event is thrown up by this conflict – the crisis itself, the announcement by Lopakhin that he has bought the estate. There is a curious air of detachment about some of the episodes. Charlotta Ivanovna's musing about her past, and the irruption of the Passer-by, seem like side-eddies at the edge of the main river. For the whole of this second act, in fact, the narrative comes to a halt. Life hangs suspended for a while in the old mode before everything finally changes, like water scarcely moving in the depths of the millpool before it plunges down the race to the wheel.

Chekhov confessed to Knipper that he had been 'scared' himself by the 'lack of movement' in Act Two. So was Stanislavsky when he saw it in rehearsal. 'For a long time the play was not working,' he wrote later. 'Particularly the second act. It contains no action, in the theatrical sense, and at rehearsals seemed very monotonous. It was essential to show the boredom of doing nothing in a way that was interesting.' He asked for cuts. Chekhov did more than cut; he rearranged and rewrote. (The material that came out can be found in A Note on the Translation.) The cuts were restored in Mike Alfreds's production of the play at the National Theatre, but this seems to me quite wrong. The alterations went into the original production only a month after it had opened when it was already an established success. It is difficult to believe that Chekhov would have made them at that stage if he had not fully concurred in them himself. But they shed a little more light on several of the characters. Charlotta Ivanovna has a good line about Ranyevskaya – 'She's perpetually mislaying things. She's mislaid her life, even.' And Firs is more plainly seen as what he is – a peasant, an ex-serf, rather than a kind of Russian Jeeves.

Two other characters have in the past been much misunderstood by directors. Natural sympathy for the Gayev family and their feckless charm has sometimes obscured the qualities of

Lopakhin and Trofimov, the representatives of economic and political progress who are, in their different ways, pushing them to the margins of life. ('Suddenly no one needs us any more,' as Gayev sadly discovers in Act Four, when the money has gone.) They both feel genuine love for their unintended victims, and Chekhov's letters make it clear that he took a characteristically objective view of both of them. 'Lopakhin is a businessman, it's true,' he wrote to Stanislavsky, conscious of the way in which progressive prejudice was likely to work, 'but he is in every sense a decent person. He must behave with complete decorum and propriety, without pettiness or trickery . . . In casting this part it must be kept in mind that Lopakhin has been loved by Varya, a serious and religious young lady; she wouldn't have fallen in love with some grasping peasant.'

Trofimov has suffered in different ways. In the past he has sometimes been portrayed in English productions as an inadequate and immature personality who is afraid to emerge from university and face the real world. This view has been given currency by the translation which has become traditional for his ironic description of himself – 'the eternal student', a phrase that suggests in English not only the correct primary meaning of remaining a student forever, but also (as in 'the eternal schoolboy' or 'the eternal triangle') the idea of his being the unchanging student *type*. The Russian phrase, *vyechniy studyent*, has quite a different overtone; it is a variant of *vyechniy zhid*, literally 'the eternal Jew', but in English the Wandering Jew, who was condemned to wander the earth for all eternity without shelter. Chekhov makes the implication of this clear in the same letter to Knipper in which he admits to his worries about Act Two. His other anxiety, he says, is '. . . the somewhat unfinished state of the student, Trofimov. The point is that Trofimov is perpetually being exiled, perpetually being thrown out of the university – and how do you show things like this?' Exiled, of course, for his political activities; and the difficulty of showing things like this being the censor (who, even as it was, cut two passages from Trofimov's speeches – about the condition of the workers and about the effect that the ownership of serfs has had upon the Gayev family). Chekhov plainly takes Trofimov seriously as a man

who holds sane and genuine convictions for which he is prepared
to suffer. But then to go to the opposite extreme, as was done in
Trevor Griffiths's adaptation of the play, and to turn him into a
'positive hero' in the Socialist Realist sense, is also an absurdity.
Even if we had not discovered by now that Chekhov's characters
are never puppets, Trofimov and his beliefs, like Vershinin and
his, are obviously being held at some slight ironic distance. He
is plainly ridiculous when he claims to be 'above such things as
love'. Even his sincerest speeches topple into rhetoric about mankind marching towards higher truth and higher happiness. (His
excited outburst to Anya at the end of Act Two – 'On, on, on! We
are going to that bright star that blazes from afar there, and no
one can hold us back! On, on, on! In step together, friends!' –
echoes a famous revolutionary ode by Pleshcheyev, the writer to
whom Chekhov addressed his disclaimer of all political and
religious enthusiasm – 'On, on, with neither fear nor doubting/To
great and valorous feats, my friends . . .!/And like a guiding star
on high/Let blaze for us the sacred truth . . .'). He complains
about people doing nothing but talk even as he stands there doing
nothing but talk. Lopakhin and Trofimov, in fact, like all
Chekhov's characters, speak out boldly and sincerely in their own
voices. Each rises to his heights of magnanimity and understanding, and each comes up against his own particular limitations.

The greatest problem, though, in playing and understanding
The Cherry Orchard is to know whether or not it is a comedy. Are
we to laugh or are we to cry? Both, no doubt. But this is easier to
achieve in theory than in practice, and on the page rather than on
the stage. An audience is a large, corporate creature with large,
corporate emotions. It can stand close to the sufferer and feel his
pain, or it can hold him at arm's length and see the absurdity of
his helplessness; it finds it very difficult to be in both places at
once. The ambiguity of the text gives the people who have to perform it genuine practical difficulties, and they must always be
tempted to resolve them by pushing the tone in one direction or
the other.

The same problem arises with all the last four plays, and is
likely to go on puzzling directors and actors, not to mention translators, as long as they are performed. But it becomes particularly

acute in *The Cherry Orchard*. Chekhov went on insisting that it
was a 'vaudeville', even after the material had changed out of all
recognition in the writing. He designates it a comedy on the title-
page, and in his letters he said it was 'not a drama but a comedy,
in places even a farce . . .'. 'The last act will be cheerful – in fact
the whole play will be cheerful and frivolous . . .'. He was not
using these terms in some arcane private sense; the short plays
that he wrote earlier in his life are after all quite unambiguously
cheerful and frivolous, quite straightforwardly comedies, farces,
and vaudevilles.

Stanislavsky's reaction to all this was to tell Chekhov bluntly
that he was wrong. 'It's not a comedy, it's not a farce, as you
wrote,' he informed him, after everyone had wept in the last act
during the read-through at the Moscow Arts, 'it's a tragedy . . . I
wept like a woman. I tried to stop myself, but I couldn't. I can
hear you saying, "Excuse me, but it is in fact a farce . . .". No,
for the plain man it is a tragedy.'

In the past most directors seem to have agreed with Stanislavsky.
More recently the pendulum has swung the opposite way, and it
has become fashionable to establish the comic nature of all these
four plays by presenting the characters as ludicrously self-
obsessed grotesques, and by supplying sight-gags that the author
overlooked. This may be another example of the somewhat eccentric influence exercised by David Magarshack, one of the most
distinguished of Chekhov's translators. In his book *Chekhov the
Dramatist* he urges the view that *The Cherry Orchard* is simply a
funny play in its entirety. He even manages to find the last scene
funny, where Firs is left locked into the empty house for the
winter. He argues that the stage-direction says merely that Firs is
lying motionless, not dying, and that someone will shortly realise
what has happened, and come back and release him. This seems
to me frankly preposterous. No doubt Firs is not clinically dead at
the fall of the curtain, but anyone who believes he has a serious
chance of emerging from that room alive has clearly never considered the practicalities of play-writing, let alone the effects of
extreme cold upon extreme old age. In the course of the last act
Chekhov establishes not once but three times, in a brilliantly
escalating confirmation of misunderstanding, that the family

believes Firs to have been taken off to hospital already; not once but four times that the house is to be closed up for the winter; and even twice that the temperature is already three degrees below zero. If you can believe that after all this there remained in Chekhov's mind some unexpressed hope that Gayev, say, might get the next train back from town, or that Yepikhodov might for some reason suddenly take it into his head to unlock the house again and inspect its contents, then you can believe that Wagner hoped the local fire brigade might just get there in time at the end of *Götterdämmerung*.

Nor will the text as a whole support Magarshack's view. As in all the plays, something is being lost – something that will never be recovered even if all the bright prophecies of the optimists were to come true tomorrow. Those trees, that begin in blossom and end beneath the axe, are everything that ever can be lost by mortal man – childhood, happiness, purpose, love, and all the brightness of life. It is truly not possible to read the play in Russian without being moved, as Stanislavsky and his company were, to tears as well as to laughter.

Some of Chekhov's references to the play's comicality have a characteristically teasing or self-mocking air – he was deeply shocked when Stanislavsky was said to be thinking of staging one of his actual vaudevilles at the Arts Theatre. He was also engaged in a running battle with Stanislavsky over the ponderousness of his staging. With *The Cherry Orchard* he evidently feared the worst from the very beginning. 'I should very much like to be around at rehearsals to have a look,' he wrote anxiously to Nemirovich-Danchenko. 'I am afraid that Anya might have a tearful tone of voice (you for some reason find her similar to Irina) . . . Not once in my text does Anya weep, and nowhere does she speak in a tearful voice. In the second act she has tears in her eyes, but her tone of voice is cheerful and lively. Why in your telegram do you talk about there being a lot of people weeping in the play? Where are they? The only one is Varya, but that's because Varya is a crybaby by nature, and her tears are not supposed to elicit a feeling of gloom in the audience. In my text it often says "on the verge of tears", but that indicates merely the characters' mood, not tears. There is no cemetery in the second act.'

But even these quite specific comments can't be taken too literally, because they are at variance with Chekhov's own text. According to the stage-directions, Gayev is 'wiping away his tears' in Act Three. Ranyevskaya, at the end of the act, is 'weeping bitterly'. Both of them, at the end of the last act, 'sob quietly'. Part of what Chekhov wanted when he insisted on the comedy in his plays was surely a different style of playing; he was looking for lightness, speed, indifference, and irony; something that suggested not the inexorable tolling of fate but the absurdity of human intentions and the meaninglessness of events.

The Cherry Orchard, though, does seem to me to be a comedy in some sense that the other plays are not, and I think it is possible to grasp this aspect of it without losing sight of its painfulness; indeed, to see the suffering of the characters as being expressed through the comic inappropriateness of their reactions. The slothful reluctance of the Gayevs to face what is happening to them, their inability to save the ship by jettisoning the cargo, is undoubtedly comic. And Chekhov is right about the last act; it is in some sense cheerful. The crisis has occurred at the end of Act Three, as it does in *Uncle Vanya*. What it calls forth in the characters, however, is not a spirit of endurance, as it does in the earlier play, but the absurd lightening of the spirits that occurs, as Chekhov has observed with the most wonderful ironic shrewdness, after a decision has been taken, however terrible, and the worst has actually happened. It is notable that in this last play, with his own death only months away, Chekhov is struck not so much by the inexorable nature of terrible events as by their survivability, by their way of slipping out of the mind, once they have occurred, and of disappearing in the endless wash of further events.

But the cheerfulness is deeply poignant. The worst *has* happened, and it is a bad worst. The Gayevs' happiness has been irretrievably lost, as both brother and sister for one moment realise before they leave the house; and their future will be even bleaker than Nina's on her tours of second-rate provincial theatres, or Vanya's and Sonya's at the account-books of their provincial estate, or the Prozorov sisters' in their grim northern exile. A few months work at the bank for Gayev; a few months with her hopeless lover in Paris for Ranyevskaya. Then resolution and love and the last of the money will all run out. They will have neither home nor occupation; nothing. There is something absurd about their prospects, though, because the Gayevs remain too feckless to understand them; they lack the tragic dignity that Sonya and her uncle and the Prozorov sisters all muster in the end. This is why, finally, the play is a comedy. It is the comedy of inertia and helplessness in the face of truly desolating loss. There is no simple formula for playing it, or for responding to it; the problem it sets us is the problem of life itself.

MICHAEL FRAYN

A Note on the Translation

Although this is Chekhov's last play it was the first one I translated (it was commissioned for Peter Hall's production at the National Theatre in 1978). By the time it was revived in London, for the production by Sam Mendes at the Aldwych Theatre in 1989, I had discovered a little more about translating Chekhov, and I made a fair number of revisions.

I have, as always, been fairly ruthless about names. I have teased out *vyechniy studyent* (see Introduction), and attached a date to the emancipation of the serfs, which would have been as firmly located in Russian minds as (say) the Second World War in ours. I have supplied what Chekhov merely specifies in a stage-direction, the first few lines of Alexei Tolstoy's marvellously bad poem *The Scarlet Woman*, which is about a Judean courtesan who boasts that she will subdue Jesus with one of her irresistible looks, and instead is herself subdued by John the Baptist with one of his.

I am still in two minds about the scene with the Passer-by. In the original, after the words 'Wonderful weather', he 'declaims' a few words. Baldly translated they are meaningless: 'My brother, my suffering brother . . . go out to the Volga; whose groans . . .?' In fact the line consists of two quotations (or misquotations). The first half is taken from an indifferent poem by Nadson, whom I suspect, from references in the letters, Chekhov despised. The second half comes from what seems to me a rather magnificent poem by Nekrasov, *Reflections on the Gateway to a Great House*. I have supplied enough of each poem to make sense – and the sense parallels a lot of Trofimov's ideas. This makes the Passer-by's 'declamation' into rather a performance, whereas in the original he is behaving like carol-singers who give you two lines of *Hark the Herald Angel Sings*, then hold out their hand for money. I have left my extended version in the text for anyone who wants it, but on balance I think it would be better to cut it, and go straight from 'Wonderful weather' to 'Mademoiselle, spare a few kopeks for a starving Russian'.

It may, incidentally, be relevant in understanding this scene that the word for 'Passer-by', *prokhozhy*, meant in Siberian usage at that time someone who was tramping the roads to escape from prison or exile. Chekhov must have come across this usage on his journey to Sakhalin, though whether he intended any part of that sense here I do not know.

Before Chekhov rewrote Act Two after the opening in Moscow (see Introduction) Charlotta did not appear in the scene at the beginning of the act, and Trofimov did not have his two speeches at the end, where he asks Anya to have faith in him, and sees happiness coming with the rising moon. Instead the act began with a scene between Trofimov and Anya:

> YASHA *and* DUNYASHA *are sitting on the bench.* YEPIKHODOV *is standing beside it.* TROFIMOV *and* ANYA *come along the path from the estate.*

ANYA. Great-aunt is all alone in the world – she's very wealthy. She's no love for Mama. The first few days I was there I found it very hard – she didn't say much to me. Then she cheered up and started to laugh. She promised to send the money – she gave me and Charlotta some for the journey. Oh, but it's a horrible feeling, being the poor relation.

TROFIMOV. It now looks as if there's someone here already . . . Sitting on the bench. Let's go on, then.

ANYA. I was away from home for three weeks. I started to pine most dreadfully.

> TROFIMOV *and* ANYA *go out.*

Then Dunyasha says 'All the same, how lovely to spend some time abroad . . .' After Ranyevskaya's line, 'Perhaps we'll think of something,' the original text continued:

> VARYA *and* CHARLOTTA IVANOVNA *come along the path from the estate.* CHARLOTTA *is wearing a man's suit, and is carrying a gun.*

VARYA. She's a sensible, well-brought-up girl, and nothing can happen, but all the same she shouldn't be left alone with a young man. Supper at nine o'clock. Make sure you're not late.

CHARLOTTA. I'm not hungry. (*Hums quietly.*)

VARYA. It doesn't matter. You must be there for appearances' sake. Look, they're sitting over there, on the bank.

VARYA *and* CHARLOTTA IVANOVNA *go out.*

And at the end of the act, after Anya's line: 'You put it so beautifully!' the scene originally continued:

TROFIMOV. Sh . . . Someone's coming. It's that Varya again! (*Angrily.*) It's outrageous!

ANYA. Come on – let's go down to the river. It's nice there.

TROFIMOV. Come on, then.

ANYA. The moon will be rising soon.

ANYA *and* TROFIMOV *go out.*

Enter FIRS, *then* CHARLOTTA IVANOVNA. FIRS *mutters away as he looks for something on the ground near the bench. He strikes a match.*

FIRS. Oh, you sillybilly!

CHARLOTTA (*sits down on the bench and takes off her peaked cap*). Is that you, Firs? What are you looking for?

FIRS. The mistress has lost her purse.

CHARLOTTA (*searches*). Here's her fan. And here's her handkerchief – it smells of perfume. (*Pause.*) There isn't anything else. She's perpetually mislaying things. She's mislaid her life, even. (*Hums quietly.*) I haven't got proper papers – I don't know how old I am. So I think of myself as being young . . . (*Puts the cap on* FIRS, *who sits motionless.*) Oh, I love you, my dear sir! (*Laughs.*) *Ein, zwei, drei!* (*Takes the cap off* FIRS, *and puts it on herself.*) When I was a little girl, Mama and my father used to go round all the fairs . . .

And she gives what is now the opening speech of the act, down to, 'I don't know anything.' Then:

FIRS. When I was twenty, twenty-five years old, I was going along one day with the deacon's son and the cook, Vasily, and

just here, on this stone, there was a man sitting . . . a stranger –
belonged to someone else – we didn't know him . . . For some
reason I got scared, and I went off, and after I'd gone the other
two set on him and killed him . . . He'd got money on him.

CHARLOTTA. So? *Weiter!* Go on!

FIRS. So then along came the law, and they started to question us.
They took the pair of them away . . . they took me, too. I was
two years in jail . . . Then that was that, they let us go. It was a
long while back. (*Pause.*) I can't remember it all.

CHARLOTTA. An old man like you – it's time for you to die.
(*Eats the cucumber.*)

FIRS. Eh? (*Mutters to himself.*) So there they were, they all went
along together, and there they stopped . . . Uncle jumped down
from the cart . . . he picked up the sack . . . and inside that
sack was another sack. And he looks, and there's something
going twitch! twitch!

CHARLOTTA (*laughs quietly*). Twitch, twitch! (*Eats the cucumber.*)

*Someone can be heard walking quietly along the path and quietly
playing the balalaika. The moon rises. Somewhere over by the
poplars* VARYA *is looking for* ANYA.

VARYA (*calling, off*). Anya! Where are you?

Curtain.

Pronunciation of the Names

The following is an approximate practical guide. In general, all stressed a's are pronounced as in 'far' (the sound is indicated below by 'aa') and all stressed o's as in 'more' (they are written below as 'aw'). All unstressed a's and o's are thrown away and slurred. The u's are pronounced as in 'crude'; they are shown below as 'oo'.

Ranyevskaya (Lyuba, Lyubov Andreyevna) – Ranyevskaya (*Lyoob*a, Lyoo*bawf* And*ra*yevna)

Anya, Anyechka – *Aan*ya, *Aan*yechka

Varya – *Vaar*ya

Gayev (Leonid Andreyich, Lenya) –
Guy-(as in Fawkes)-yev, *Len*ya, Leo*need* And*ra*yich)

Lopakhin (Yermolay) – Lo*paakh*een (Yermo*lie* – as in 'lie' meaning 'untruth')

Trofimov (Petya) – Tro*feem*ov (*Pet*ya)

Simeonov-Pishchik – Sim*yawn*ov-*Peesh*-cheek

Charlotta Ivanovna – Shar*lawt*a Ee*vaan*ovna

Yepikhodov – Yepi*khawd*ov

Dunyasha – Doon*yaash*a

Firs – Fierce

Yasha – *Yaash*a

Anastasy – Anas*taas*y

Dashenka – *Daash*enka

Deriganov – Deri*gaan*ov

Grisha – *Greesh*a

Kardamonov – Karda*mawn*ov

Karp – Kaarp

Kharkov – *Khaar*kov

Kozoyedov (Fyodor) – Kozoyedov (*Fyaw* – dor – two syllables, not three)

Lopakhina – Lo*paakh*ina

Mama – *Maam*a

Petrushka – Pe*troosh*ka

Polya – *Pawl*ya

Ragulin – Ra*gool*in

Tolstoy (Aleksey Konstantinovich) – Tol*stoy* (Alek*say* Konstan*teen*ovich)

Yaroslavl – Yaro*slaavl*

Yashnevo – *Yaash*nevo

Yefimushka – Ye*feem*ooshka

Yegor – Ye*gawr*

Yevstigney – Yevsti*gnay*

Znoykov – *Znoy*kov

The Cherry Orchard

This translation of The Cherry Orchard *was first staged by the National Theatre in the Olivier on 3 February 1978. The cast was as follows:*

RANYEVSKAYA *(Lyuba), a landowner*	Dorothy Tutin
ANYA, *her daughter, aged 17*	Judi Bowker
VARYA, *her adopted daughter, aged 24*	Susan Fleetwood
GAYEV *(Lenya), Ranyevskaya's brother*	Robert Stephens
LOPAKHIN *(Yermolay), a businessman*	Albert Finney
TROFIMOV *(Pyetya), a student*	Ben Kingsley
SIMEONOV-PISHCHIK, *a landowner*	Terence Rigby
CHARLOTTA IVANOVNA, *the governess*	Helen Ryan
YEPIKHODOV, *the estate clerk*	Nicky Henson
DUNYASHA, *the chambermaid*	Susan Littler
FIRS, *the footman, an old man of 87*	Ralph Richardson
YASHA, *the young footman*	Derek Thompson
A PASSER-BY	Peter Needham
THE STATIONMASTER	Daniel Thorndike

Directed by Peter Hall
Designed by John Bury

The action takes place on Ranyevskaya's estate.

This revised translation of The Cherry Orchard *was produced by Michael Codron and staged at the Aldwych Theatre, London on 24 October 1989, with the following cast:*

DUNYASHA, *the chambermaid*	Abigail McKern
LOPAKHIN (Yermola), *a businessman*	Bernard Hill
YEPIKHODOV, *the estate clerk*	Tom Watt
FIRS, *the footman*	Michael Gough
ANYA, *Ranyevskaya's daughter*	Miranda Foster
RANYEVSKAYA (Lyuba), *a landowner*	Judi Dench
CHARLOTTA IVANOVNA, *the governess*	Kate Duchêne
VARYA, *Ranyevskaya's adopted daughter*	Lesley Manville
GAYEV (Lenya), *Ranyevskaya's brother*	Ronald Pickup
SIMEONOV-PISCHIK, *a landowner*	Barry Stanton
YASHA, *the young footman*	John Dougall
TROFIMOV (Petya), *a student*	Nicholas Farrell
A PASSER-BY	Tom Hollander
THE STATIONMASTER	Stanley Page
THE POSTMASTER	Peter Sowerbutts
PARTY GUESTS	Kate Anthony
	Patricia Samuels

Directed by Sam Mendes
Designed by Paul Farnworth

Act One

A room which is still known as the nursery. One of the doors leads to ANYA's *room. Half-light, shortly before sunrise. It is May already, and the cherry trees are in blossom, but outside in the orchard it is cold, with a morning frost. The windows are closed.*

Enter DUNYASHA *with a candle, and* LOPAKHIN *with a book in his hand.*

LOPAKHIN. God be praised, the train's arrived. What time is it?

DUNYASHA. Nearly two o'clock. (*Extinguishes the candle.*) It's light already.

LOPAKHIN. So the train's how late? Two hours, at least. (*Yawns and stretches.*) Fine one I am. Complete fool. Came all the way here to go and meet them at the station, and then just dropped off while I was sitting there. It's a shame. You might have woken me.

DUNYASHA. I thought you'd gone. (*Listens.*) That sounds like them now.

LOPAKHIN (*listens*). No . . . Luggage to pick up, one thing and another . . .

   Pause.

She's lived abroad for five years – I don't know what she'll be like now . . . She's a fine woman. Easy, straightforward. I remember, when I was a boy of fifteen or so, my father – he kept a shop then in the village here – dead now, of course – he punched me in the face, and the blood started to pour out of my nose . . . For some reason we'd come into the yard here together, and he was drunk. It seems like yesterday. She was only young – such a slim young thing. She brought me in and she took me to the washstand in this room, in the nursery.

'Don't cry, my little peasant,' she says. 'It'll heal in time for
your wedding . . .'

Pause.

My little peasant . . . it's true, my father was a peasant – and
here am I in a white waistcoat and yellow shoes. Like a pig in a
pastry-cook's . . . The only difference is I'm a rich man, plenty
of money, but look twice and I'm a peasant, a real peasant . . .
(*Leafs through the book.*) I was reading this book. Couldn't
understand a word. Fell asleep over it.

Pause.

DUNYASHA. And the dogs, they haven't slept all night. They can
sense that the mistress is coming.
LOPAKHIN. What's the matter with you, Dunyasha?
DUNYASHA. My hands are all of a tremble. I'm going to faint.
LOPAKHIN. Very tender plant, aren't you, Dunyasha? Dress like
a lady, do your hair like one, too. Not the way, is it? You want
to remember who you are.

Enter YEPIKHODOV *with a bouquet. He is wearing a jacket and
highly polished boots that squeak loudly. As he comes in he drops
the bouquet.*

YEPIKHODOV (*picks up the bouquet*). The gardener sent them. He
says to put them in the dining-room. (*Gives the bouquet to*
DUNYASHA.)
LOPAKHIN. And bring me some kvass.
DUNYASHA. Very good. (*Goes out.*)
YEPIKHODOV. Three degrees of frost this morning, and the
cherry all in blossom. I can't give our climate my seal of
approval. (*Sighs.*) Indeed I can't. It never knows how to lend a
helping hand at the right moment. And I mean look at me – I
bought myself these boots the day before yesterday, and they
squeak so much, I mean it's quite impossible. I mean, put it like
this – what should I grease them with?

LOPAKHIN. Leave off, will you? Pester, pester.

YEPIKHODOV. I don't know. Every day some disaster happens to me. Not that I complain. I'm used to it. I even smile.

Enter DUNYASHA. *She gives* LOPAKHIN *his kvass.*

YEPIKHODOV. I'll go, then. (*Stumbles against the table, which falls over.*) There you are ... (*As if exulting in it.*) You see what I'm up against! I mean, it's simply amazing! (*Goes out.*)

DUNYASHA. To tell you the truth, he's proposed to me.

LOPAKHIN. Ah!

DUNYASHA. I don't know *what* to say ... He's all right, he doesn't give any trouble, it's just sometimes when he starts to talk – you can't understand a word of it. It's very nice, and he puts a lot of feeling into it, only you can't understand it. I quite like him in a way, even. He's madly in love with me. He's the kind of person who never has any luck. Every day something happens. They tease him in our part of the house – they call him Disasters by the Dozen ...

LOPAKHIN (*listens*). I think they're coming.

DUNYASHA. They're coming! What's the matter with me? I've gone all cold.

LOPAKHIN. They are indeed coming. Let's go and meet them. Will she recognize me? Five years we haven't seen each other.

DUNYASHA (*in agitation*). I'll faint this very minute ... I will, I'll faint clean away!

Two carriages can be heard coming up to the house. LOPAKHIN *and* DUNYASHA *hurry out.*

The stage is empty. Then there is noise in the adjoining rooms. Across the stage, leaning on his stick, hurries FIRS, *who has gone to the station to meet the mistress. He is wearing ancient livery and a top hat. He is saying something to himself, but not a word of it can be made out. The noise offstage grows louder and louder.*

A VOICE (*off*). This way, look.

Enter RANYEVSKAYA, ANYA, *and* CHARLOTTA IVANOVNA, *who has a little dog on a lead. All three ladies are dressed for travelling :* VARYA *in an overcoat and shawl;* GAYEV, SIMEONOV-PISHCHIK, LOPAKHIN, DUNYASHA *with a bundle and an umbrella,* SERVANTS *carrying things – they all go across the room.*

ANYA. This way. Mama, do you remember which room this is?

RANYEVSKAYA (*joyfully, on the verge of tears*). The nursery!

VARYA. So cold. My hands are quite numb. (*To* RANYEVSKAYA.) Your rooms – the white one and the mauve one – they've stayed just as they were, Mama.

RANYEVSKAYA. The nursery. My own dear room, my lovely room . . . I slept in here when I was a little girl. (*Weeps.*) And now I'm like a little girl again . . . (*Kisses her brother, then* VARYA, *then her brother once more.*) And Varya's just the same as before – she looks like a nun. And Dunyasha I recognize . . . (*Kisses her.*)

GAYEV. The train was two hours late. What do you think of that? What kind of standards do these people have?

CHARLOTTA (*to* PISHCHIK). My dog can eat nuts even.

PISHCHIK (*surprised*). Would you believe it!

They all go out except ANYA *and* DUNYASHA.

DUNYASHA. We waited and waited . . . (*She takes off* ANYA'S *coat and hat.*)

ANYA. I didn't sleep on the way – I haven't slept for four nights . . . Oh, I'm completely frozen!

DUNYASHA. You went away in Lent, with snow on the ground still, and now look at it. Oh, my dear! (*Laughs and kisses her.*) I've waited and waited for you. My own precious! My heart's delight . . .! I'm going to tell you at once – I can't contain myself another minute . . .

ANYA (*inertly*). Nothing else.

DUNYASHA. Yepikhodov – you know who I mean, the estate clerk – just after Easter he proposed to me.

ANYA. Still on about the same old thing . . . (*Tidying her hair.*) I've gradually lost all the pins . . .

She is completely exhausted – unable to keep her balance, even.

DUNYASHA. I don't know *what* to think. He's in love with me, so in love with me!

ANYA (*looks into her room, tenderly*). My room, my windows, just as if I'd never been away. I'll get up in the morning, I'll run out into the orchard . . . Oh, if only I could get to sleep! I didn't sleep all the way – I was worn out with worry.

DUNYASHA. The day before yesterday Mr. Trofimov arrived.

ANYA (*joyfully*). Petya!

DUNYASHA. He's sleeping in the bath-house – he's living out there. He said he was afraid of being in the way. (*Looks at her pocket watch.*) We ought to wake him up, but Miss Varya said not to. Don't you go waking him, she says.

Enter VARYA, *with a bunch of keys on her belt.*

VARYA. Dunyasha, quick now – Mama's asking for coffee.

DUNYASHA. Very good. (*Goes out.*)

VARYA. Well, God be praised, you've got here, both of you. You're home again, Anya. (*Cuddling her.*) My darling's come home! My lovely's come home again!

ANYA. I've had a most terrible time.

VARYA. I can imagine.

ANYA. I set out from here in Holy Week. It was cold. Charlotta talked the whole way – she kept showing me conjuring tricks. Why on earth you saddled me with Charlotta . . .

VARYA. You couldn't have travelled alone, my darling. Not at seventeen!

ANYA. Anyway, we get to Paris, and it's cold, it's snowing. My French is terrible. Mama's living up on the fifth floor, and when I arrive she's got people with her – Frenchmen, I don't know who they were, and ladies, and some ancient Catholic priest holding a prayer-book – and the air's full of tobacco smoke, and it's bleak and uncomfortable. And suddenly I felt sorry for Mama. I felt so sorry for her I put my arms round her and pressed her head against me and couldn't let go. After that Mama kept hugging me, and crying . . .

VARYA (*on the verge of tears*). Don't, don't . . .

ANYA. She'd already sold that villa she had outside Menton. She's nothing left, nothing. Nor have I – not a kopeck. We scarcely managed it here. And Mama doesn't understand! We'll sit down to dinner in a station restaurant, and she orders the most expensive item on the menu. Then she tips all the waiters a ruble each. Charlotta's the same. And Yasha has to be fed, too – it's simply frightful. You know Mama has this footman, Yasha. We brought him with us.

VARYA. I've seen the rogue.

ANYA. So what – have we paid the interest?

VARYA. How could we?

ANYA. Oh God, oh God . . .

VARYA. In August they're going to sell the estate off.

ANYA. Oh God . . .

LOPAKHIN (*looks in at the door, and moos*). M-e-e-e . . . (*Goes out.*)

VARYA (*through her tears*). Oh, I'd like to give him such a . . . (*Raises her fist threateningly.*)

ANYA (*embraces* VARYA – *quietly*). Varya, has he proposed?

>   VARYA *shakes her head.*

Look, he loves you . . . Why don't you get things straight between you? What are you both waiting for?

VARYA. I'll tell you what I think – I think nothing's going to come of it. He's very busy, he hasn't got time for me – he doesn't even notice. Well, good luck to him, but I can't bear the sight of him. Everyone talks about our wedding, everyone keeps congratulating me, but in fact there's nothing there – it's all a kind of dream. (*In a different tone.*) You've got a bumble-bee brooch.

ANYA (*sadly*). Mama bought it. (*Goes into her room, and speaks cheerfully, childishly.*) And in Paris I went up in an air-balloon!

VARYA. Oh, my darling's come home! My lovely's come home again!

DUNYASHA is back with the coffee-pot. She makes the coffee. VARYA stands by the door to ANYA's room.

Oh, my darling, I go about the house all day in a dream. If we could just get you married to some rich man, then I could be easy in my mind. I could take myself off into a retreat, then to Kiev, to Moscow, and oh, I'd walk all round the holy places . . . I'd just keep walking and walking. The glory of it!

ANYA. The birds are singing in the orchard. What time is it now?

VARYA. It must be after two. Time for you to sleep, my darling. (*Going in to ANYA.*) The glory of it!

Enter YASHA with a rug and travelling bag.

YASHA (*crosses with delicacy*). All right to come through?

DUNYASHA. I shouldn't even recognize you, Yasha. You've changed so abroad!

YASHA. Mm . . . And who are you?

DUNYASHA. When you left I was so high . . . (*Indicates from the floor.*) Dunyasha. Fyodor Kozoyedov's daughter. You don't remember!

YASHA. Mm . . . Quite a pippin, aren't you? (*Looks round and embraces her. She screams and drops a saucer.*)

Exit YASHA, swiftly.

VARYA (*in the doorway, displeased*). Now what's going on?

DUNYASHA (*through her tears*). I've smashed the saucer . . .

VARYA. That's good luck.

ANYA (*coming out of her room*). We should warn Mama – Petya's here.

VARYA. I gave orders not to wake him.

ANYA (*reflectively*). Six years since Father died, and only a month later that Grisha was drowned in the river. My brother . . . Seven years old, and such a pretty boy. Mama couldn't bear it. She escaped – fled without so much as a backward glance . . . (*Shivers.*) I understand her so well, if only she knew!

Pause.

And Petya Trofimov was Grisha's tutor. He may remind her . . .

Enter FIRS, *in jacket and white waistcoat.*

FIRS (*goes to the coffee-pot, preoccupied*). The mistress will be taking it in here . . . (*Puts on white gloves.*) The coffee ready? (*To* DUNYASHA, *sternly.*) What's this, girl? Where's the cream?

DUNYASHA. Oh, my Lord . . . (*Rushes out.*)

FIRS (*busies himself about the coffee-pot*). Oh, you sillybilly! (*Mutters to himself.*) Come from Paris . . . The master went to Paris once . . . by post-chaise . . . (*Laughs.*)

VARYA. What are you going on about, Firs?

FIRS. What do you want? (*Joyfully.*) My lady has come home! I waited for her! I can die happy . . . (*Weeps with joy.*)

Enter RANYEVSKAYA, GAYEV, LOPAKHIN and SIMEONOV-PISHCHIK *who is wearing a tight-fitting, long-waisted coat in a fine material, and wide, Oriental-looking trousers.* GAYEV, *as he comes in, makes movements with his arms and trunk as if he were playing billiards.*

RANYEVSKAYA. How did it go? Let's see . . . Yellow into the corner. Then off the cushion into the middle pocket.

GAYEV. And screw back into the corner! There was a time, my sister, when you and I slept in this very room. And now I'm fifty-one already, strange as it seems.

LOPAKHIN. Yes, the time goes by.

GAYEV. Who?

LOPAKHIN. I say the time goes by.

GAYEV. It reeks of cheap scent in here, though.

ANYA. I'm going to bed. Good night, Mama. (*Kisses her mother.*)

RANYEVSKAYA. My beloved child. (*Kisses her hands.*) Are you pleased to be home? I don't think I shall ever manage to come down to earth.

ANYA. Good night, Uncle.

GAYEV (*kisses her face and hands*). The Lord guard and keep you. How like your mother you are! (*To his sister.*) Lyuba, at her age you were just like that.

> ANYA *gives her hand to* LOPAKHIN *and* PISHCHIK, *then goes out and closes the door behind her.*

RANYEVSKAYA. She's tired out.

PISHCHIK. It's a long way to go, no doubt about it.

VARYA (*to* LOPAKHIN *and* PISHCHIK). Well, then, gentlemen. Past two o'clock. Time to be saying goodbye.

RANYEVSKAYA (*laughs*). Varya, you're just the same as ever. (*Draws her close and kisses her.*) I'll drink my coffee, then we'll all go.

> FIRS *puts a cushion under her feet.*

Thank you, my dear. I've got into the coffee habit. I drink it day and night. Thank you, my dear old friend. (*Kisses* FIRS.)

VARYA. I must see if they've brought all the things. (*Exits.*)

RANYEVSKAYA. Is this really me sitting here? (*Laughs.*) I feel like leaping into the air and waving my arms about. (*Covers her face with her hands.*) Perhaps it's all a dream. Oh, but I love my country, God knows I do, I love it tenderly. I couldn't look out of the carriage window – I did nothing but weep. (*On the verge of tears.*) However, the coffee has to be drunk. Thank you, Firs, thank you, my dear. I'm so glad to find you still alive.

FIRS. The day before yesterday.

GAYEV. His hearing's going.

LOPAKHIN. I have to leave straight away, before five o'clock. I'm off to Kharkov. Such a shame. I just wanted to get a look at you, have a few words ... You're still as magnificent as ever.

PISHCHIK (*breathes hard*). You've grown even more lovely ... Dressed in Paris fashions ... I could throw caution to the winds.

LOPAKHIN. In the eyes of your sort – your brother here, for instance – I'm a boor, I'm a money-grubbing peasant, but I don't give a damn about that. The only thing I want is for you to trust me as you did before, to see your amazing, heart-breaking eyes looking at me the way they used to. Merciful God! My father was a serf, and your father and grandfather owned him. But you – yes, you were the one – you did so much for me once that I've forgotten all that, and I love you like my own flesh and blood ... more than my own flesh and blood.

RANYEVSKAYA. I can't sit still. I'm physically incapable ... (*Jumps up and walks about in a state of great emotion.*) I shall never survive this joy ... Laugh at me, I'm such a fool ... My bookcase, my own dear bookcase ... (*Kisses the bookcase.*) My dear old table.

GAYEV. Nanna died while you were away.

RANYEVSKAYA (*sits and drinks coffee*). Yes, God rest her soul. They wrote and told me.

GAYEV. And Anastasy died. Petrushka – you remember him? With the squint? He left me. Living in town now, working for the local police inspector. (*He takes a box of fruit-drops out of his pocket and sucks one.*)

PISHCHIK. My daughter Dashenka – she sends her best regards ...

LOPAKHIN. I want to tell you some very pleasant and cheering news. (*Glances at his watch.*) I shall be leaving very shortly, we haven't time for a proper talk ... I'll put it in two words, then. You know, of course, that your cherry orchard is to be sold to pay your debts – the sale is fixed for the twenty-second of August. But don't you worry yourself about it, my dear – sleep easy in your bed at night – there is a way out ... This is my plan. Now listen carefully. Your estate is only thirteen miles out of town; the railway has now come through right next to it; and if the cherry orchard and the land along the river are broken up into building lots and leased out as sites for summer cottages, then you will possess an income of – at the very least – twenty-five thousand rubles a year.

GAYEV. I'm sorry, but it's such nonsense!

RANYEVSKAYA (*to* LOPAKHIN). I don't entirely understand you.

LOPAKHIN. You will get from your leaseholders at the very minimum ten rubles a year per acre. And if you advertise it now, then I swear upon anything you like to name that by the autumn you won't have a single acre left – it will all have been taken up. In short – congratulations, you're saved. It's a marvellous position with this deep river. The only thing, of course, is that you need to tidy it up a bit. Remove all the old buildings, for example – like this house, which won't have any use now – and cut down the old cherry orchard.

RANYEVSKAYA. Cut it down? My dear, forgive me, but you don't understand. If there is one thing of any interest at all in this whole province – if there is even something rather remarkable – then it's our cherry orchard.

LOPAKHIN. There's only one thing remarkable about this orchard. It's very big. You only get a full crop every other year, and then there's nothing to do with it – no one buys it.

GAYEV. There's even a reference to this orchard in the encyclopaedia.

LOPAKHIN (*glances at his watch*). If we don't think of something, if we don't come to some decision, then on the twenty-second of August not only the cherry orchard but the whole estate will be sold at auction. So nerve yourselves! There is no other way out, I swear to you. None whatsoever.

FIRS. In the old days, forty, fifty years ago, they used to dry the cherries, they used to soak them, they used to pickle them, they used to make jam out of them, and year after year . . .

GAYEV. Do be quiet, Firs.

FIRS. And year after year they'd send off dried cherries by the cartload to Moscow and Kharkov. There was money then! And the dried cherries were soft and juicy and sweet and scented . . . They knew the recipe in those days.

RANYEVSKAYA. And what's happened to this recipe now?

FIRS. They've forgotten it. No one remembers it.

PISHCHIK (*to* RANYEVSKAYA). How was it in Paris, then? Did you eat frogs?

RANYEVSKAYA. I ate crocodiles.

PISHCHIK. Would you believe it!

LOPAKHIN. Up to now in the countryside we've had only the gentry and the peasants. But now a new class has appeared – the summer countrymen. Every town now, even the smallest, is surrounded with summer cottages. And we may assume that over the next twenty years or so our summer countryman will be fruitful and multiply exceedingly. Now he merely sits on his verandah and drinks tea, but you know it may come to pass that he'll put his couple of acres to some use, and start to cultivate them. And then this old cherry orchard of yours will become happy and rich and luxuriant . . .

GAYEV (*exasperated*). Such nonsense!

Enter VARYA *and* YASHA.

VARYA. Mama, there are two telegrams that came for you. (*Selects a key which clinks in the lock as she opens the antique bookcase.*) Here.

RANYEVSKAYA. From Paris. (*Tears up the telegrams without reading them.*) Paris is over and done with.

GAYEV. But, Lyuba, do you know how old this bookcase is? I pulled out the bottom drawer last week, and I looked, and there were some numbers burnt into the wood with a poker. This bookcase was built exactly one hundred years ago. What do you think of that? We could celebrate its centenary. It's an inanimate object, but all the same, whichever way you look at it, it's still a bookcase.

PISHCHIK (*in surprise*). A hundred years ... Would you believe it!

GAYEV. Yes ... Quite an achievement ... (*Feels the bookcase.*) Dear bookcase! Most esteemed bookcase! I salute your existence, which for more than a hundred years now has been directed towards the shining ideals of goodness and of truth. For a hundred years your unspoken summons to fruitful labour has never faltered, upholding, (*on the verge of tears*) through all the generations of our family, wisdom and faith in a better future, and fostering within us ideals of goodness and of social consciousness.

Pause.

LOPAKHIN. Yes ...

RANYEVSKAYA. You're the same as ever, Lenya.

GAYEV (*in some slight confusion*). In off into the righthand corner! Then screw back into the middle pocket!

LOPAKHIN (*glances at his watch*). Well, I must be on my way.

YASHA (*hands pills to* RANYEVSKAYA). Take your pills now, perhaps ...

PISHCHIK. Dearest heart, you mustn't go taking medicines ... there's neither harm nor charm in them ... Give them here ... Dear lady. (*Picks up the pills, tips them out on to his palm, blows on them, puts them into his mouth, and washes them down with kvass.*) There!

RANYEVSKAYA (*alarmed*). But you've gone utterly mad!

PISHCHIK. I've taken all the pills.

LOPAKHIN. There's a greedyguts!

Everyone laughs.

FIRS. When he was here at Easter he put away half a bucket of pickled cucumbers ... (*Mutters.*)

RANYEVSKAYA. What's he going on about now?

VARYA. He's been muttering away like this for the last three years. We've got used to it.

YASHA. Old age, isn't it?

> CHARLOTTA IVANOVNA *crosses the stage, in a white dress. She is very thin and very tightly laced, with a lorgnette hanging from her belt.*

LOPAKHIN. Forgive me, I haven't had a chance to say hello to you. (*Tries to kiss her hand.*)

CHARLOTTA (*taking her hand away*). Let you kiss my hand, and next thing I know you'll be after my elbow, then my shoulder...

LOPAKHIN. Not having any luck today, am I?

> *Everyone laughs.*

Come on, then, show us a conjuring trick!

CHARLOTTA. No, I just want to go to bed. (*Goes out.*)

LOPAKHIN. Well, we'll meet again in three weeks time. (*Kisses* RANYEVSKAYA'*s hand.*) So until then. (*To* GAYEV.) Goodbye. (*Exchanges kisses with* PISHCHIK.) Goodbye. (*Gives his hand to* VARYA, *then to* FIRS *and* YASHA.) I only wish I didn't have to go. (*To* RANYEVSKAYA.) If you come to a decision about the houses, let me know, and I'll get you fifty thousand on account. Think about it seriously.

VARYA (*angrily*). Oh, go *on*!

LOPAKHIN. I'm going, I'm going. (*Exits.*)

GAYEV. A boor – the man's a boor. Oh, *pardon*... Varya's going to marry him. He's Varya's intended.

VARYA. Uncle, please, don't start.

RANYEVSKAYA. Why, Varya, I shall be very happy. He's a good man.

PISHCHIK. A most – it has to be said – worthy man. And my Dashenka ... she also says that, well, she says various things. (*Snores, but immediately wakes up again.*) But all the same, dear lady, if you could oblige me ... with a loan of two hundred and forty rubles ... The interest on my mortgage is due tomorrow ...

VARYA (*alarmed*). No, no!

RANYEVSKAYA. I really do have nothing.

PISHCHIK. Well, it'll get itself found somehow. (*Laughs.*) I never lose hope. Here we are, I think to myself, everything's lost, I'm done for – but not at all, because lo and behold – the railway's come through my land, and . . . they've paid me. And by and by, you'll see, one day soon, something else will happen . . . There's two hundred thousand Dashenka's going to win – she's got a lucky ticket.

RANYEVSKAYA. The coffee's finished. We can go to bed.

FIRS (*brushes* GAYEV; *lecturing*). You've put the wrong trousers on again. What am I to do with you?

VARYA (*quietly*). Anya's asleep. (*Quietly opens a window.*) The sun's up already – it's not cold. Look, Mama – what marvellous trees they are! And oh, sweet heavens, the air! And the starlings are chattering!

GAYEV (*opens another window*). The orchard's all in white. You haven't forgotten, Lyuba? The way the long avenue there runs straight, straight, like a ribbon stretched taut, the way it shines on moonlit nights. You remember? You haven't forgotten?

RANYEVSKAYA (*looks out of the window at the orchard*). Oh, my childhood, my innocence! In this nursery I slept, from this room I looked out at the orchard, and happiness woke with me every morning. The orchard was just the same then, nothing has changed. (*Laughs with joy.*) All, all in white! Oh, my orchard! After dark foul autumn and cold cold winter, again you're young and filled with happiness, and not abandoned by the angels. If only the millstone could be lifted from my neck. If only I could forget my past!

GAYEV. Yes, even the orchard will be sold to meet our debts. Strange as it seems . . .

RANYEVSKAYA. Look – there's Mama, our own dead Mama, walking through the orchard . . . in a white dress! (*Laughs with joy.*) It's her.

GAYEV. Where?

VARYA. God save you, Mama.

RANYEVSKAYA. There's no one there. It just looked like it for a moment. To the right, on the turning to the summer-house – a tree bending under its blossom like the figure of a woman.

Enter TROFIMOV, *in a shabby student's uniform and spectacles.*

What an amazing orchard it is! The white masses of the blossom, the pale blue of the sky . . .

TROFIMOV. Lyubov Andreyevna!

She looks round at him.

I'm just going to pay my respects to you, and then I'll go away and leave you in peace. (*Ardently kisses her hand.*) I was told to wait until morning, but I didn't have patience enough.

RANYEVSKAYA *gazes at him in perplexity.*

VARYA (*on the verge of tears*). It's Petya.

TROFIMOV. Trofimov. Petya Trofimov. I used to be Grisha's tutor . . . Have I really changed so much?

RANYEVSKAYA *embraces him and weeps quietly.*

GAYEV (*embarrassed*). Come on, Lyuba. Come on, now.

VARYA (*weeps*). Petya, I did tell you to wait until tomorrow.

RANYEVSKAYA. My Grisha . . . my boy . . . Grisha . . . my son . . .

VARYA. What can we do, Mama? It was God's will.

TROFIMOV (*softly, on the verge of tears*). There now . . . There, now . . .

RANYEVSKAYA (*weeps quietly*). My boy died, my little boy was drowned . . . Why? Why, my friend? (*More quietly.*) Anya's asleep in there, and here am I talking at the top of my voice . . . making a noise . . . What's this, Petya? Why have you lost your looks? Why have you aged so?

TROFIMOV. You know what some old woman on a train the other day called me? – 'That mangy-looking gentleman.'

RANYEVSKAYA. You were still only a boy before, just a nice

young student. Now you've got glasses, your hair's gone thin. You're surely not still a student? (*Goes to the door.*)

TROFIMOV. I should think I'm going to be a perpetual student. The Wandering Student, like the Wandering Jew.

RANYEVSKAYA (*kisses her brother, then* VARYA). Well, off to bed, then . . . You've aged, too, Leonid.

PISHCHIK (*follows her*). So, bedtime . . . Oh, my gout. I'll stay the night here, I think. (*To* RANYEVSKAYA.) And in the morning, dearest heart, if you would . . . two hundred and forty rubles . . .

GAYEV. Never gives up, does he?

PISHCHIK. Two hundred and forty rubles . . . I have to pay the interest on my mortgage.

RANYEVSKAYA. I have no money, my sweet.

PISHCHIK. I'll give it back, my dear. It's the most piffling sum.

RANYEVSKAYA. Well, all right. Leonid will give it to you. You give it to him, Leonid.

GAYEV. If it's up to me, he can whistle for it.

RANYEVSKAYA. What can we do? Just give it to him . . . He needs it . . . He'll give it back.

Exeunt RANYEVSKAYA, TROFIMOV, PISHCHIK *and* FIRS.

GAYEV, VARYA *and* YASHA *remain.*

GAYEV. My sister still hasn't got out of the habit of flinging her money around. (*To* YASHA.) Do go away, my dear good chap – you smell of chickens.

YASHA (*grinning*). And you're just the same as you always were.

GAYEV. Who? (*To* VARYA.) What does he say?

VARYA (*to* YASHA). Your mother's come from the village. She's been sitting in the servants' hall since yesterday waiting to see you.

YASHA. Well, good luck to her, then.

VARYA. Shameless, aren't you?

YASHA. What's the point. She could just as well have come tomorrow. (*Goes out.*)

VARYA. Mama's exactly the same as she was. She hasn't changed at all. If it was up to her she'd have given everything away.

GAYEV. Yes . . .

Pause.

If for some disease a great many different remedies are proposed, then it means that the disease is incurable. I think, I cudgel my brains – I have many remedies, a great many – and what that means when you get down to it is that I haven't a solitary one. It would be a good thing if we got an inheritance from someone. It would be a good thing if we married Anya to some very rich man. It would be a good thing if we went to Yaroslavl and tried our luck with that aunt of ours, the countess. She's very rich indeed, you know.

VARYA (*weeps*). If only God would help.

GAYEV. Don't howl. Aunt is very rich, but she doesn't like us. In the first place, my sister married an ordinary lawyer instead of a gentleman with property . . .

ANYA *appears in the doorway.*

She married a commoner, and the way she's behaved – well, you couldn't say it was very virtuously. She's good, she's kind, she's a splendid woman, I love her dearly, but however many extenuating circumstances you think up, the fact has to be faced: she is depraved. You can sense it in her slightest movement.

VARYA (*in a whisper*). Anya is standing in the doorway.

GAYEV. Who?

Pause.

Funny – I've got something in my right eye. I can't see properly. And on Thursday, when I was at the district court . . .

Enter ANYA.

VARYA. Why aren't you asleep, Anya?

ANYA. I can't get to sleep.

GAYEV. My pet. (*Kisses* ANYA's *face and hands.*) My child . . . (On the verge of tears.) You're not my niece – you're my angel. You're everything to me. Believe me. Trust me.

ANYA. I trust you, uncle. Everyone loves you, everyone looks up to you . . . but, dear Uncle, you must be quiet, only be quiet. What were you saying just then about my mother – about your own sister? Why did you say that?

GAYEV. Yes, yes . . . (*Covers his face with her hand.*) Really, that was terrible! God forgive me! And today I made a speech to the bookcase . . . so stupid! And only when I'd finished did I realize how stupid it was.

VARYA. It's true, Uncle dear, you must keep quiet. Just be quiet, that's all.

ANYA. If you're quiet, you'll be calmer in yourself, too.

GAYEV. I am silent. (*Kisses their hands.*) Not a word. Just one thing on a matter of business. On Thursday I was at the district court, and, well, a few of us there got talking about this and that, one thing and another, and it seems it would be possible to arrange a loan against my note of hand to pay the bank interest.

VARYA. If only the Lord would help!

GAYEV. On Tuesday I'll go and have another talk about it. (*To* VARYA.) Don't howl. (*To* ANYA.) Your mother will have a word with Lopakhin. He obviously won't refuse her. And you – as soon as you've got your breath back you'll go to Yaroslavl to see the countess, your great aunt. So we'll be operating from three sides at once – and the job's as good as done. We shall pay the interest, of that I'm convinced. (*Puts a fruit drop in his mouth.*) I swear, upon my honour, upon whatever you like, that the estate will not be sold! (*Excitedly.*) By my hope of happiness I swear it! Here's my hand on it – call me a low, dishonourable fellow if I let it go to auction! By my whole being I swear to you!

ANYA (*her calm mood has returned to her: she is happy*). What a good man you are, Uncle, what a good and clever man! (*Embraces him.*) Now I'm calm! Quite calm! I'm happy!

Enter FIRS.

FIRS (*to* GAYEV, *reproachfully*). What? Have you no fear before God? When are you going to bed?

GAYEV. Right now, right now. You go off. Don't worry about me, I'll undress myself. Well, night night, then, children. Details tomorrow, but now to bed. (*Kisses* ANYA *and* VARYA.) I am a man of the eighties. Not a period they speak well of these days, but I can tell you that I have suffered not a little in this life for my convictions. It's no accident that your ordinary peasant loves me. You have to know your peasant! You have to know how to . . .

ANYA. Uncle, you're off again!

VARYA. Dear uncle, just be quiet.

FIRS (*angrily*). Leonid Andreyich!

GAYEV. I'm coming, I'm coming . . . Off to bed, then. Cushion, cushion, and into the middle pocket! Clean as a whistle . . . (*Goes out, with* FIRS *trotting behind him.*)

ANYA. Now I'm calm. I don't want to go to Yaroslavl – I don't like our great aunt. But all the same I'm calm. Thanks to Uncle. (*Sits down.*)

VARYA. We must get some sleep. I'm off. One rather annoying thing happened while you were away, though. You know what used to be the servants' quarters? Well, of course, it's only the elderly servants who live there now: Yefimushka, Polya, Yevstigney, oh, yes, and Karp. Well, they began to let various riff-raff in to spend the night. I said nothing about it. Only then I hear they've been spreading a rumour to the effect that I've had them fed on nothing but dried peas. Out of meanness, do you see . . . And all this is Yevstigney's doing . . . Right, I think to myself. If that's the way you want it, then just you wait. So I send for Yevstigney . . . (*Yawns.*) He comes in . . .

What's all this, then, Yevstigney? I say to him . . . You're such a fool . . . (*Looks at* ANYA.) Anyechka . . .!

Pause.

Asleep . . .! (*Takes* ANYA *by the arm.*) Off we go to bed, then . . . Off we go . . .! (*Leads her.*) My poor precious has fallen fast asleep! Off we go . . .

A long way away, beyond the orchard, a SHEPHERD *plays on a reed pipe.*

TROFIMOV *crosses the stage, and stops at the sight of* VARYA *and* ANYA.

VARYA. Sh . . . She's asleep . . . asleep . . . Off we go, my own sweet precious.

ANYA (*quietly, half asleep*). So tired . . . I can still hear the harness bells . . . Uncle . . . dear Uncle . . . Mama and Uncle, too . . .

VARYA. Off we go, my own sweet love. Off we go . . .

They go into ANYA's *room.*

TROFIMOV (*moved*). My sunshine! My springtime!

CURTAIN

Act Two

The open fields. A wayside shrine – old, crooked, and long neglected. Beside it – a well, large slabs which were evidently once tombstones, and an old bench. A path can be seen leading to the Gayev estate. At one side rise the dark shapes of poplars; this is where the cherry orchard begins.

In the distance is a row of telegraph poles, and a long way away on the horizon a large town can just be made out, visible only in very fine, clear weather. The sun is just about to set.

CHARLOTTA, YASHA and DUNYASHA are sitting on the bench; YEPIKHODOV is standing beside it, playing the guitar. They are all in a reflective mood.

CHARLOTTA is wearing an old peaked cap. She has taken a gun off her shoulder and is adjusting the buckle on the sling.

CHARLOTTA (*meditatively*). I haven't got proper papers – I don't know how old I am. So I always think of myself as being young. When I was a little girl Mama and my father used to go round all the fairs giving shows. Very good shows they were, too. And I'd turn somersaults and do all kinds of little tricks. And when Papa and Mama died, some German lady took me in and began to give me an education. So, all right, I grew up, and then I went to be a governess. But where I come from and who I am, I don't know. Who my parents were – whether they were even married or not – I don't know. (*Gets a cucumber out of her pocket and eats it.*) I don't know anything.

Pause.

I so long to talk to someone, but there's no one to talk to. I haven't got anyone.

YEPIKHODOV (*plays the guitar and sings*).
> *What should I care for life's clamour,*
> *What for my friend or my foe . . .*

How very agreeable it is to pluck at the strings of a mandoline!

DUNYASHA. That's not a mandoline – that's a guitar. (*Powders herself in a pocket mirror.*)

YEPIKHODOV. For the madman who's in love it's a mandoline. (*Sings.*)
> *. . . Had I a passion requited*
> *Warming my heart with its glow?*

YASHA *joins in.*

CHARLOTTA. Horrible way these people sing! Faugh! Like jackals howling!

DUNYASHA (*to* YASHA). All the same, how lovely to spend some time abroad.

YASHA. Yes, of course. I couldn't agree more. (*Yawns, and then lights a cigar.*)

YEPIKHODOV. Oh, absolutely. Everything abroad's been in full constitution for years.

YASHA. Obviously.

YEPIKHODOV. Here am I – I mean, I'm a grown man – I read – I read all sorts of important books – but what I can't make out is any I mean kind of movement of opinion when it comes to what I personally want in life. Put it this way – do I want to go on living, or do I want to shoot myself? I mean, I always carry a revolver on me, look. (*Shows the revolver.*)

CHARLOTTA. Done it. I'm off. (*Slings the gun on her shoulder.*) Yepikhodov, you're a genius. A terrifying genius. All the women ought to be mad about you. Brrr! (*Starts to go.*) These great brains – they're all such fools. I've no one to talk to. Alone, always alone, I haven't got anyone. And who I am and why I am remains a mystery . . . (*Goes unhurriedly off.*)

YEPIKHODOV. I mean, leaving everything else aside, I mean just taking my own case, and I'm not going to mince my words, but, really, fate has treated me quite relentlessly. I've been tossed around like a rowing-boat in a high sea. All right, let's say I'm talking nonsense. In that case, why, just to take one example, why, when I woke up this morning, why did I find, sitting there on my chest, this enormous spider? Like this. (*Demonstrates with both hands.*) All right, take another example. I pour myself some kvass, to have a drink, and there in the glass is something really profoundly horrible. I mean, a cockroach, for example.

Pause.

Have you read Buckle? The History of Civilization?

Pause

(*To* DUNYASHA.) If I might trouble you, I should appreciate the chance of a word or two.

DUNYASHA. Go on, then.

YEPIKHODOV. I should have been hopeful of having it in private. (*Sighs.*)

DUNYASHA (*embarrassed*). All right – only first fetch me my cloak. You'll find it by the cupboard. It's rather damp here.

YEPIKHODOV. Now I know what to do with my revolver . . . (*Takes his guitar and goes off playing it.*)

YASHA. Poor old Disasters! Between you and me, that man is a fool. (*Yawns.*)

DUNYASHA. Just so long as he doesn't go and shoot himself.

Pause.

I've got so nervy these days – I worry all the time. They took me into service when I was a little girl still. I've got out of the way of ordinary people's life now. Look at my hands – white as white, like a lady's. I've turned into someone all refined, someone terribly delicate and ladylike – I'm frightened of everything. It's dreadful being like this. And Yasha, if you deceive me, well, I don't know what would become of my nerves.

YASHA (*kisses her*). Real country pippin, aren't you? Of course, every girl's got to remember who she is. If there's one thing I hate more than anything else, it's a girl who doesn't know how to behave herself.

DUNYASHA. I'm absolutely passionately in love with you. Because you're an educated man – you can talk about anything.

Pause.

YASHA (*yawns*). Right . . . What I think is, if a girl's in love with someone then she's got no morals.

Pause.

Nice having a cigar in the open air . . . (*Listens.*) Someone coming . . . It's *them*.

DUNYASHA *impetuously embraces him.*

Go home as if you'd been down to the river for a swim – here, along this path. Otherwise you'll run into them and they'll think I've been seeing you. I'm not having that.

DUNYASHA (*coughs quietly*). Your cigar's given me a headache . . . (*Goes off.*)

YASHA *remains, sitting beside the shrine.*

Enter RANYEVSKAYA, GAYEV, *and* LOPAKHIN.

LOPAKHIN. It has to be settled once and for all – time won't wait. Look, it's a simple enough question. Do you agree to lease out the land for summer cottages or not? Answer me one word: yes or no? Just one word!

RANYEVSKAYA. Who's smoking some foul cigar? (*Sits.*)

GAYEV. It's very convenient now they've built the railway. (*Sits.*) We popped into town and had some lunch . . . Yellow into the middle pocket! I should have gone indoors first and had a quick game.

RANYEVSKAYA. You've still got time.

LOPAKHIN. Just one word! (*Pleading.*) Give me an answer!

GAYEV (*yawns*). Who?

RANYEVSKAYA (*looks into her purse*). There was a lot of money in here yesterday, and today there's hardly any. My poor Varya feeds everyone on milk soup to economize – she gives the old men in the kitchen nothing but dried peas, while I somehow just go on mindlessly spending . . . (*Drops the purse and scatters gold coins.*) And now it's gone everywhere . . . (*She is annoyed.*)

YASHA. Leave it to me – I'll do it. (*Picks up the coins.*)

RANYEVSKAYA. Would you, Yasha? And why did I go into town for lunch? That horrible restaurant of yours with the music playing, and the tablecloths smelling of soap . . . Why do you drink so much, Lenya? Why do you eat so much? Why do you talk so much? In the restaurant today you kept talking again – and it was all so rambling. The seventies, the Decadent movement. And who were you saying it all to? Fancy telling the waiters about the Decadents!

LOPAKHIN. Yes.

GAYEV (*waves his hand*). I'm incorrigible, that's obvious. (*To* YASHA, *irritated.*) What is it? You're perpetually dangling in front of my eyes.

YASHA (*laughs*). I can't hear your voice without wanting to laugh.

GAYEV (*to his sister*). Either he goes, or I do.

RANYEVSKAYA. Off you go, Yasha.

YASHA (*gives* RANYEVSKAYA *her purse*). Certainly. (*Scarcely restrains himself from laughing.*) This instant. (*Goes.*)

LOPAKHIN. Your estate is going to be bought by Deriganov. He's a very wealthy man. I gather he's coming to the sale in person.

RANYEVSKAYA. Where did you hear that?

LOPAKHIN. It's what they're saying in town.

GAYEV. Our aunt in Yaroslavl has promised to send something, but when and how much – that we don't know.

LOPAKHIN. What would it be? A hundred thousand? Two hundred thousand?

RANYEVSKAYA. Ten or fifteen thousand, and lucky if we get even that.

LOPAKHIN. Forgive me for saying this, but such frivolous people as you, such strange unbusinesslike people, I have never come across. You are told in plain language that your estate is being sold, and you simply do not understand.

RANYEVSKAYA. What can we possibly do? Tell us.

LOPAKHIN. I tell you every day. Every day I tell you exactly the same thing. The cherry orchard and the land along the river must be leased out for summer cottages – and it must be done now, as soon as possible – the sale is upon us! Get it into your heads! Just once make up your minds to have the houses and you will get money – as much money as you like – and you will be saved.

RANYEVSKAYA. Summer cottages – summer people – forgive me, but it's so squalid.

GAYEV. I agree entirely.

LOPAKHIN. I don't know whether to scream, or to burst into tears, or to fall down in a faint. I can't go on! You reduce me to despair! (*To* GAYEV.) You're an old woman!

GAYEV. Who?

LOPAKHIN. An old woman. You! (*Starts to go.*)

RANYEVSKAYA (*frightened*). No, don't go. Stay with us, my dear. I beg you. Perhaps we'll think of something.

LOPAKHIN. What is there to think of?

RANYEVSKAYA. Don't go, I implore you. It's more fun with you here, at any rate . . .

Pause.

I keep waiting for something to happen – as if the house were going to come down about our ears.

GAYEV (*deep in thought*). Red, cushion, and into the corner . . . Cushion, red, and into the corner . . .

RANYEVSKAYA. We have sinned, and sinned greatly . . .

LOPAKHIN. What are your sins, then?

GAYEV (*puts a fruit drop in his mouth*). They say I've wasted all
my substance in fruit drops . . . (*Laughs.*)

RANYEVSKAYA. Oh, my sins . . . Always I've thrown money
about like a lunatic, and I married a man who made nothing of
his life but debts. My husband died of champagne – he was a
terrible drinker – and my misfortune then was to fall in love
with someone else. I gave myself to him, and it was just at that
time – and this was my first punishment, it was like a club
coming down on my head – my little boy . . . in the river here
. . . my little boy was drowned, and I went away, went abroad,
went utterly away, went meaning never to return, never to see
this river again . . . I shut my eyes, ran blindly – and *he* after
me . . . pitilessly, brutally. I bought a villa outside Menton,
because *he* fell sick there, and for three years I knew no rest,
neither by day nor by night. For three years he was an invalid –
he drained my strength – my spirit broke. And last year, when
the villa was sold to pay my debts, I went to Paris, and there
he robbed me openly, he threw me aside, he took up with
another woman. I tried to poison myself . . . So stupid, so
shameful . . . And suddenly I yearned for Russia, for my
homeland, for my daughter . . . (*Wipes her tears.*) Lord, Lord
have mercy! Forgive me my sins! Don't punish me any more!
(*Takes a telegram out of her pocket.*) I got this today from
Paris . . . He begs my forgiveness, implores me to return . . .
(*Tears the telegram up.*) There's a sound of music somewhere.
(*Listens.*)

GAYEV. That's our famous Jewish orchestra. Do you remember?
Four fiddles, flute, and double bass.

RANYEVSKAYA. It still exists? We ought to get them here somehow – we ought to arrange an evening.

LOPAKHIN (*listens*). I can't hear anything . . .
(*Sings quietly.*)
> Money talks, so here's poor Russkies
> Getting Frenchified by Germans.

(*Laughs.*) Very good play I saw last night. Very funny.

RANYEVSKAYA. There's nothing funny in the world. People shouldn't watch plays. They should look at their own selves a little more often. What grey lives they all lead. How much they say that should never be said at all.

LOPAKHIN. True. We live like complete fools, it has to be admitted.

Pause.

My father was a peasant. He was an idiot, he knew nothing, he taught me nothing, all he did was to take his stick to me when he was drunk. And when you get down to it, I'm just the same sort of stupid oaf myself. I've never learnt anything. I write such a foul hand I'm ashamed for people to see it. I'm a pig.

RANYEVSKAYA. What you need, my friend, is to get married.

LOPAKHIN. Yes . . . That's true.

RANYEVSKAYA. To Varya, why not? Our own Varya. She's a good girl.

LOPAKHIN. Yes.

RANYEVSKAYA. She came to me from simple people – she works the whole day long. But the main thing is, she loves you. Yes, and you've liked her for a long time now.

LOPAKHIN. Fair enough. I've nothing against it. She's a good girl.

Pause.

GAYEV. I've been offered a job in a bank. Six thousand a year. Have you heard about that?

RANYEVSKAYA. The idea! You just stay as you are.

Enter FIRS. *He has brought an overcoat.*

FIRS (*to* GAYEV). Now will you put it on, sir, if you please, or you'll be getting damp.

GAYEV (*puts on the coat*). Firs, my friend, you're a bore.

FIRS. No call for that, now. You went off this morning without a word. (*Examines him.*)

RANYEVSKAYA. You've aged, Firs, haven't you?

FIRS. What do you want?

LOPAKHIN. She says you've aged a lot!

FIRS. I've lived a long life. They were marrying me off before your Papa even arrived in the world. (*Laughs.*) And when the Freedom came, in sixty-one, I was already head valet. I didn't agree to have the Freedom – I stayed with the masters . . .

Pause.

And I remember, everyone was glad. But what they were glad about they didn't know themselves.

LOPAKHIN. Lovely it was before. At least they flogged you.

FIRS (*not having heard right*). Oh, my word, they were. The peasants belonged to the masters, and the masters to the peasants. Now it's all chippety-choppety – you can't make any sense of it.

GAYEV. Do be quiet for a moment, Firs. Tomorrow I have to go into town. I've been promised an introduction to a general who might put up something against my note of hand.

LOPAKHIN. Nothing's going to come of it, whatever you do. And you're not going to pay that interest, don't worry.

RANYEVSKAYA. He's living in a dream. There's no general.

Enter TROFIMOV, ANYA *and* VARYA.

GAYEV. Some more of us coming.

ANYA. It's Mama.

RANYEVSKAYA (*tenderly*). Here . . . here . . . my own darlings . . . (*Embracing* ANYA *and* VARYA.) If only you knew how much I love you both! Sit next to me – here . . .

They all settle themselves down.

LOPAKHIN. Our Wandering Student always seems to be wandering with the young ladies.

TROFIMOV. Mind your own business.

LOPAKHIN. He'll be fifty before he knows where he is, and still a student.

TROFIMOV. Why don't you leave off your stupid jokes?

LOPAKHIN. Not losing your temper, are you, O weird one?

TROFIMOV. Don't keep badgering me.

LOPAKHIN (*laughs*). All right, then, my dear sir. What do you make of me?

TROFIMOV. I'll tell you what I make of you, sir. You're a wealthy man – you'll soon be a millionaire. And just as there must be predatory animals to maintain nature's metabolism by devouring whatever crosses their path, so there must also be you.

They all laugh.

VARYA. Petya, I think it would be better if you told us about the planets.

RANYEVSKAYA. No, let's go on with the conversation we were having yesterday.

TROFIMOV. What was that about?

GAYEV. Pride.

TROFIMOV. We talked for a long time yesterday, but we never arrived at any conclusions. Human pride, in the sense you're using it, has some kind of mystical significance. And you may even be right, in your own fashion. But if we're going to talk about it in a down-to-earth way, without any fancy trimmings, then what sort of pride can there be – does the expression have any sense at all – if man is physiologically ill-constructed, if in the vast majority of cases he is crude and stupid and profoundly unhappy? We have to stop admiring ourselves. We have simply to work.

GAYEV. It makes no difference – you still die.

TROFIMOV. Who knows? And what does it mean – you die? Perhaps man has a hundred senses, and at death it's only the five we know of that perish, while the other ninety-five go on living.

RANYEVSKAYA. What a clever man you are, Petya!

LOPAKHIN (*ironically*). Oh, staggeringly.

TROFIMOV. Mankind is advancing, perfecting its powers. All the things that are beyond its reach now will one day be brought close and made plain. All we have to do is to work, to bend all our strength to help those who are seeking the truth. Here in Russia very few as yet are working. Most members of the intelligentsia, so far as I know it, are seeking nothing, neither the truth nor anything else. They're doing nothing – they're still incapable of hard work. They call themselves the intelligentsia, but they treat servants like children, and peasants like animals. They don't know how to study. They never do any serious reading. They understand next to nothing about art; science they merely talk about. They're all terribly serious people with terribly stern expressions on their faces. They all talk about nothing but terribly important questions. They all philosophize away. And right in front of their eyes the whole time there are workers living on filthy food and sleeping without pillows to their heads, thirty and forty to a room – and everywhere bugs, damp, stench, and moral squalor. And all the fine conversations we have are plainly just to distract attention from it all. Our own attention, and other people's, too. Show me – where are the crèches that everyone's always going on about – where are the reading-rooms? They're only in novels – they don't exist in reality. There's just filth and banality and barbarism. I have little love for all those serious faces; I fear those serious conversations. Better to be silent.

LOPAKHIN. Listen, I get up before five every morning, I work all the hours God gave, I'm constantly handling money – my own and other people's – and I can't help seeing what my fellow men are like. You've only got to start trying to do something to discover how few honest, decent people there are in the world. Sometimes, when I can't sleep, I think to myself: 'Lord, you gave us immense forests, boundless plains, broad horizons – living in it all we ought properly to be giants.'

RANYEVSKAYA. A lot of use giants would be. They're all right in fairy-tales. Anywhere else they're frightening.

YEPIKHODOV crosses upstage, playing the guitar.

(*Pensively.*) There goes Yepikhodov . . .
ANYA (*likewise*). There goes Yepikhodov . . .
GAYEV. The sun has set, ladies and gentlemen.
TROFIMOV. Yes.
GAYEV (*softly, as if declaiming*). O nature, wondrous nature! You shine with an everlasting radiance, beautiful and indifferent; you that we call Mother unite within yourself existence and death; you give life and you destroy it . . .
VARYA (*imploringly*). Uncle!
ANYA. You're doing it again!
TROFIMOV. You'd be better off potting yellow.
GAYEV. I am silent, I am silent.

They all sit lost in thought. Silence. All that can be heard is FIRS *muttering quietly. Suddenly there is a distant sound, as if from the sky: the sound of a breaking string – dying away, sad.*

RANYEVSKAYA. What was that?
LOPAKHIN. I don't know. Somewhere a long way off, in the mines, a winding cable has parted. But a long, long way off.
GAYEV. Perhaps a bird of some sort . . . something like a heron.
TROFIMOV. Or some kind of owl.
RANYEVSKAYA (*shivers*). Horrible, I don't know why.

Pause.

FIRS. It was the same before the troubles. The owl screeched, and the samovar moaned without stop.
GAYEV. Before what troubles?
FIRS. Before the Freedom.

Pause.

RANYEVSKAYA. Listen, my friends, we must be going. The night is drawing on. (*To* ANYA.) There are tears in your eyes. What is it, child? (*Embraces her.*)

ANYA. Nothing. Just tears. It doesn't matter.

TROFIMOV. There's someone coming.

A PASSER-BY *appears. He is wearing an overcoat and a stolen white peaked cap; he is slightly drunk.*

PASSER-BY. Begging your pardon – can I get through this way to the station?

GAYEV. Yes. Along this path.

PASSER-BY. Most profoundly grateful. (*Coughs.*) Wonderful weather . . . (*Declaims.*)

> My friend, my brother, weary, suffering, sad,
> Though falsehood rule and evil triumph,
> Take courage yet and let your soul be glad . . .

Pause.

> Go to the Volga. Hear again
> The song it sings, the song of groans –
> The litany of hauling men,
> Groaned from weary hearts and bones.
> Volga! All spring's melted snows,
> And still you cannot flood your plain
> As wide as this land overflows
> With all its people's sea of pain . . .

(*To* VARYA) Mademoiselle, spare a few kopeks for a starving Russian.

VARYA *is frightened, and cries out.*

LOPAKHIN (*angrily*). Now that's enough! There are limits!

RANYEVSKAYA (*hurriedly*). Wait . . . here you are . . . (*Looks in her purse.*) I've no silver . . . Never mind, here – ten rubles . . . (*Gives him a gold coin.*)

PASSER-BY. Most profoundly grateful. (*Goes off.*)

Laughter.

VARYA (*frightened*). I'm going in . . . Oh, Mama – at home there's nothing for the servants to eat, and you gave him ten rubles.

RANYEVSKAYA. What's to be done with me? – I'm so silly! When we get home I'll give you everything I've got. (*To* LOPAKHIN.) You'll lend me some more, won't you?

LOPAKHIN. Your humble servant.

RANYEVSKAYA. Ladies and gentlemen, it's time we were going. Oh, and Varya, while we were sitting here we quite made a match for you. So congratulations.

VARYA (*on the verge of tears*). Don't joke about it, Mama.

LOPAKHIN. Get thee to a nunnery, Ophelia-Ophoolia.

GAYEV. My hands are shaking – I've been missing my billiards.

LOPAKHIN. Nymph, in thy orisons be all my sins dismembered!

RANYEVSKAYA. Off we go, then. It's nearly time for supper.

VARYA. He gave me such a fright. My heart's simply pounding.

LOPAKHIN. Let me remind you, ladies and gentlemen: the cherry orchard will be coming up for sale on the twenty-second of August. Think about it! Think!

They all go out except TROFIMOV *and* ANYA.

ANYA (*laughing*). We ought to thank that tramp for frightening Varya. Now we're alone.

TROFIMOV. She's afraid you and I are suddenly going to fall in love with each other. She doesn't let us out of her sight for days at a time. What she can't get into her narrow mind is that we're above such things as love. Our whole aim – the whole sense of our life – is to avoid the petty illusions that stop us being free and happy. On, on, on! We are going to that bright star that blazes from afar there, and no one can hold us back! On, on, on! In step together, friends!

ANYA (*clasping her hands*). How beautifully you talk!

Pause.

It's wonderful here today.

TROFIMOV. Yes, amazing weather.

ANYA. What have you done to me, Petya? Why don't I love the cherry orchard like I used to? I loved it so tenderly. I thought there was nowhere finer on earth.

TROFIMOV. All Russia is our orchard. The earth is broad and beautiful. There are many marvellous places.

Pause.

Think for a moment, Anya: your grandfather, your great-grandfather – all your forebears – they were the masters of serfs. They owned living souls. Can't you see human faces, looking out at you from behind every tree-trunk in the orchard – from every leaf and every cherry? Can't you hear their voices? The possession of living souls – it's changed something deep in all of you, hasn't it. So that your mother and you and your uncle don't even notice you're living on credit, at the expense of others – at the expense of people you don't allow past the front hall . . . We're two hundred years behind the times at least. We still have nothing – no properly defined attitude to the past. We just philosophize away, and complain about our boredom or drink vodka. But it's only too clear that to start living in the present we have to redeem our past – we have to break with it. And it can be redeemed only by suffering, only by the most un'ieard-of, unceasing labour. You must understand that, Anya.

ANYA. The house we live in hasn't been ours for a long time now. I'm going to leave, I give you my word.

TROFIMOV. Throw the keys down the well, and go. Be free as the wind.

ANYA (*in delight*). You put it so beautifully!

TROFIMOV. Have faith in me, Anya! Have faith in me! I'm not thirty yet – I'm young – I'm still a student – but I've borne so much already! Every winter I'm hungry, sick and fearful, as poor as a beggar. And the places I've been to! The places where fate has driven me! And all the time, at every minute of the day and night, my soul has been filled with premonitions I can't explain or describe. I have a premonition of happiness, Anya. I can just see it now . . .

ANYA (*pensively*). The moon is rising.

There is the sound of YEPIKHODOV *still playing the same mournful song on his guitar. The moon rises. Somewhere over by the poplar trees* VARYA *is looking for* ANYA.

VARYA (*calling off*). Anya! Where are you?

TROFIMOV. Yes, the moon is rising.

Pause.

Here it is – happiness. Here it comes. Closer and closer. I can hear its footsteps already. And if we don't see it, if we never know its face, then what does it matter? Others will!

VARYA (*off*). Anya! Where are you?

TROFIMOV. There's that Varya again! (*Angrily.*) It's outrageous!

ANYA. Come on – let's go down to the river. It's nice there.

TROFIMOV. Come on, then.

They start to go.

VARYA (*off*). Anya! Anya!

CURTAIN

Act Three

The drawing-room, with an archway leading through into the ball-room. The chandelier is lit.

From an ante-room comes the sound of the Jewish orchestra mentioned in Act Two. Company has been invited for the evening. In the ballroom they are dancing the 'grand-rond'.

SIMEONOV-PISHCHIK (*off*). *Promenade à une paire!*

> *The* COUPLES *emerge into the drawing-room – first* PISHCHIK *and* CHARLOTTA IVANOVNA, *second* TROFIMOV *and* RANYEVSKAYA, *third* ANYA *and the* POSTMASTER, *fourth* VARYA *and the* STATIONMASTER, *and so on.* VARYA *is quietly weeping, and wiping her eyes as she dances. In the last couple is* DUNYASHA. *They go round the room.*

PISHCHIK. *Grand-rond balancez . . .! Les cavaliers à genoux et remerciez vos dames!*

> FIRS, *wearing a tailcoat, brings the seltzer water on a tray.* PISHCHIK *and* TROFIMOV *come into the drawing-room.*

PISHCHIK. Blood-pressure – that's my trouble. I've had two strokes already, and I don't find dancing easy. But you know what they say – if you run with the pack you must wag your tail. I'm as strong as a horse. My late father, who was something of a humourist, God rest his soul, used to say the venerable tribe of Simeonov-Pishchik was descended from the horse that Caligula made consul . . . (*Sits down.*) But the snag is – no money! What do people say? – A hungry dog believes only in meat . . . (*Snores and immediately wakes up again.*) Same with me – can't think about anything but money.

TROFIMOV. It's true – there is something rather horse-like about you.

PISHCHIK. Well, that's all right . . . a horse is a good beast . . . a horse can be sold.

There is the sound of billiards being played in the next room. VARYA *appears in the archway to the ballroom.*

TROFIMOV (*teasing*). Madame Lopakhina! Madame Lopakhina!
VARYA (*angrily*). And who's this? The mangy-looking gentleman.
TROFIMOV. Yes, that's what I am – a mangy-looking gentleman. And proud of it!
VARYA (*reflecting bitterly*). Here we are, we've hired musicians – but what are we going to pay them with? (*Goes out.*)
TROFIMOV (*to* PISHCHIK). If all the energy you've expended during your life in the quest for money had gone on something else, you could have turned the world upside down by now.
PISHCHIK. Nietzsche – the philosopher – very great philosopher, very famous one – man of enormous intelligence – he claims in his books that it's all right to forge banknotes.
TROFIMOV. You've read Nietzsche, have you?
PISHCHIK. Well . . . my daughter Dashenka was telling me about him. Though with the position I'm in now, even if I started forging banknotes . . . I've got to pay three hundred and ten rubles the day after tomorrow . . . I've got hold of a hundred and thirty . . . (*Feels his pockets in alarm.*) The money's gone! I've lost the money! (*On the verge of tears.*). Where's the money? (*Joyfully.*) Here it is, in the lining . . . I'd quite come out in a sweat.

Enter RANYEVSKAYA *and* CHARLOTTA IVANOVNA.

RANYEVSKAYA (*hums a Caucasian dance, the lezghinka*). Why is Leonid taking so long? What can he be doing in town? (*To* DUNYASHA.) Dunyasha, ask the musicians if they'd like some tea.
TROFIMOV. The sale probably never took place.
RANYEVSKAYA. It wasn't the moment to have the band, it wasn't

the moment to get up a ball. Well, who cares? (*Sits down and hums quietly.*)

CHARLOTTA (*offers* PISHCHIK *a pack of cards*). Think of a card. Any card you like.

PISHCHIK. I've thought of one.

CHARLOTTA. Now shuffle the pack. Good. Give it to me, then, my dear monsieur Pishchik. *Ein, zwei, drei!* Now have a look and you'll find it in your side pocket.

PISHCHIK (*gets a card out of his side pocket*). The eight of spades – that's absolutely right! (*Amazed.*) Well, would you believe it!

CHARLOTTA (*to* TROFIMOV, *holding the pack in the palm of her hand*). The top card – quick – what is it?

TROFIMOV. I don't know . . . oh . . . the queen of spades.

CHARLOTTA. Right! (*To* PISHCHIK.) Well? The top card?

PISHCHIK. The ace of hearts.

CHARLOTTA. Right! (*Claps her hands, and the pack disappears.*) Marvellous weather we're having!

A mysterious female voice answers, apparently from under the floor.

VOICE. Oh, yes, wonderful weather!

CHARLOTTA. You are my heart's ideal!

VOICE. Yes, I've taken rather a fancy to you.

STATIONMASTER (*applauds*). Madame the ventriloquist! Bravo!

PISHCHIK (*amazed*). Would you believe it! Enchanting woman! I've absolutely fallen in love with you.

CHARLOTTA. In love? (*Shrugs her shoulders.*) Are you really capable of love? *Guter Mensch, aber schlechter Musikant.*

TROFIMOV (*claps* PISHCHIK *on the shoulder*). You're so much like a horse, you see . . .

CHARLOTTA. Your attention please. One more trick. (*Takes a travelling rug off one of the chairs.*) I have here a very fine rug, a very fine rug for sale. (*Shakes it.*) Who'll buy this very fine rug?

PISHCHIK (*amazed*). Would you believe it!

CHARLOTTA. *Ein, zwei, drei!* (*She has lowered the rug; now she quickly raises it.*)

ANYA *is standing behind the rug. She curtseys, runs to her mother and embraces her, then runs back into the ballroom amid general delight.*

RANYEVSKAYA (*applauds*). Bravo, bravo . . .!

CHARLOTTA. Once more, now! *Ein, zwei, drei!* (*Raises the rug.*)

VARYA *is standing behind the rug. She bows.*

PISHCHIK (*amazed*). Would you believe it!

CHARLOTTA. And that is the end of my show. (*Throws the rug at* PISHCHIK, *curtseys, and runs out into the ballroom.*)

PISHCHICK (*hurries after her*). What a witch, though! What a witch! (*Goes.*)

RANYEVSKAYA. And still no sign of Leonid. I don't understand what he could be doing in town for all this time. It must be over by now. Either the estate is sold, or else the sale never took place. What's the point of keeping us all in suspense?

VARYA (*trying to calm her*). Uncle has bought it – I'm sure of that.

TROFIMOV (*sarcastically*). Oh, of course he has.

VARYA. Great-aunt gave him authority to purchase it in her name, and to transfer the mortgage to her. It was all for Anya's sake. And, God willing, I'm sure Uncle will have done it.

RANYEVSKAYA. To buy this estate – and to buy it in her own name, because she doesn't trust us – your great-aunt sent fifteen thousand rubles – not enough even to pay the interest. (*Covers her face with her hands.*) Today my fate is being decided. My fate . . .

TROFIMOV (*teases* VARYA). Madame Lopakhina!

VARYA (*angrily*). The Wandering Student! They've thrown you out of university twice already.

RANYEVSKAYA. Why are you getting so cross, Varya? All right, he's teasing you about Lopakhin – but what of it? If you want to marry Lopakhin, then marry him. He's a good man, he's an interesting person. If you don't want to, then don't. Darling, no one's forcing you.

VARYA. I must tell you, Mama, that this is something I take very seriously. He's a good man, and I like him.

RANYEVSKAYA. Then marry him. Why wait? I don't understand.

VARYA. Mama dear, I can't propose to *him*. For two years now everyone's been talking to me about him. Everyone's been talking except him. He either says nothing or else makes a joke of it. I see why. He's busy making his fortune – he's no time for me. If only we had some money – just a little, a hundred rubles even – I'd throw up everything, I'd go away. I'd go into a nunnery.

TROFIMOV. The glory of it!

VARYA (*to* TROFIMOV). I thought students were supposed to have a little sense in their heads! (*In a gentle voice, with tears in her* (*eyes.*) Oh, but Petya, you've grown so ugly, you've aged so! (*To* RANYEVSKAYA, *no longer crying.*) It's just that I can't manage without things to do, Mama. Every minute of the day I must have something to do.

Enter YASHA.

YASHA (*scarcely restraining himself from laughing*). Yepikhodov's broken the billiard cue . . .! (*Goes out.*)

VARYA. What's Yepikhodov doing here? Who said he could play billiards? I simply don't understand these people. (*Goes out.*)

RANYEVSKAYA. Don't tease her, Petya. You can see, she's unhappy enough as it is.

TROFIMOV. She's very diligent, I must say that for her. Particularly at minding other people's business. All summer she's given me and Anya no peace. She's been frightened we were going to have some kind of romance. What's it to do with her?

Particularly since I've shown not the slightest sign of it – I'm not given to that sort of vulgarity. We're above such things as love!

RANYEVSKAYA. I suppose I must be beneath them. (*In great anxiety.*) Why isn't Leonid back? If only I knew whether the estate was sold or not. It seems such an incredible disaster that I just can't think – I can't keep control of myself . . . I could scream as I stand here . . . I could do something quite foolish. Save me, Petya. Talk to me about something, talk to me . . .

TROFIMOV. Does it make any difference whether the estate's been sold today or not? All that was finished with long ago – there's no way back – the path's grown over. Be calm now, my dear. Don't deceive yourself. Face up to the truth for once in your life.

RANYEVSKAYA. Yes, but what truth? You can see which is truth and which is falsehood, but I feel as if I'd gone blind – I can't see anything at all. You boldly settle all the great questions, but my love, isn't that because you're young, isn't that because you've never had to live a single one of those questions out? You look boldly forwards, but isn't that because you have the eyes of youth, because life is still hidden from them, so that you see nothing frightening in store? You're more daring than the rest of us, you're deeper, you're more honest – but think about it for a moment, be just a touch magnanimous in your judgment, take pity on me. After all, I was born here, my father and mother lived here, my grandfather . . . I love this house. Without the cherry orchard I can't make sense of my life, and if it really has to be sold, then sell me along with it . . . (*Embraces* TROFIMOV, *and kisses him on the forehead.*) And then this is where my son was drowned . . . (*Weeps.*) You're a good man, a kind man – have pity on me.

TROFIMOV. You know I sympathize with all my heart.

RANYEVSKAYA. Yes, but not said like that, not like that . . . (*Takes out her handkerchief, and a telegram falls on the floor.*)

There is such a weight upon my heart today, you can never know. All this noise here – my heart jumps at every sound – everything in me jumps. But to go away and be on my own – I can't, because as soon as I'm alone and surrounded by silence I'm terrified. Don't judge me, Petya. I love you as if you were my own child. I should have been glad to let you marry Anya – I truly should. Only, my precious boy, you must study, you must finish at university. It's so strange – you do nothing but get yourself tossed by fate from one place to the next. Isn't that true? Yes? And you must do something with your beard somehow to make it grow. (*Laughs.*) You are an absurd man!

TROFIMOV (*picks up the telegram*). I've no desire to be known for my looks.

RANYEVSKAYA. It's a telegram from Paris. Every day they come. One yesterday, another one today. That wild man – he's ill again, he's in trouble again. He begs my forgiveness, he implores me to come, and really I ought to go to Paris, I ought to be with him. You're pulling your stern face, Petya, but my dear, what can I do, what can I possibly do? He's ill, he's lonely and unhappy, and who'll look after him there, who'll keep him from making mistakes, who'll give him his medicine at the right time? And what's the point of hiding it or not talking about it? – I plainly love him. I love him, love him. He's a millstone round my neck – he'll take me to the bottom with him. But I love this millstone of mine – I can't live without it. (*Presses* TROFIMOV's *hand.*) Don't think harsh thoughts, Petya. Don't say anything to me. Don't speak.

TROFIMOV (*on the verge of tears*). Forgive me if I'm frank, please God forgive me, but listen – he's openly robbed you!

RANYEVSKAYA. No, no, no, you mustn't say things like that . . . (*Covers her ears.*)

TROFIMOV. Look, he's no good, and you're the only one who doesn't know it! He's a petty scoundrel, a nobody . . .

RANYEVSKAYA (*angry now, but restraining it*). You're twenty-six, twenty-seven years old, and you're still a schoolboy, you're still a fifth-former.

TROFIMOV. If you say so.

RANYEVSKAYA. It's time you were a man. At your age you must understand people who know what it is to love. You must know what it is yourself! You must fall in love! (*Angrily.*) Yes, yes! You're no more pure than I am! You're just a prig, a ridiculous freak, a monster . . .!

TROFIMOV (*in horror*). What is she saying?

RANYEVSKAYA. 'I'm above such things as love!' You're not above anything – you're merely what our Firs calls a sillybilly. Fancy not having a mistress at your age!

TROFIMOV (*in horror*). This is appalling! What is she saying? (*Rushes towards the ballroom, holding his head.*) Appalling . . . I can't cope with this, I shall have to go . . . (*Goes out, but immediately comes back.*) Everything is finished between us! (*Goes out into the anteroom.*)

RANYEVSKAYA (*calls after him*). Petya, wait! You absurd man! I was joking! Petya!

In the anteroom someone can be heard rushing downstairs, and then suddenly falling with a crash. ANYA *and* VARYA *cry out, but then at once there is a sound of laughter.*

What's happening out there?

ANYA *runs in.*

ANYA (*laughing*). Petya's fallen downstairs! (*Runs out.*)

RANYEVSKAYA. What a freak that Petya is . . .

The STATIONMASTER *takes up a position in the middle of the ballroom.*

STATIONMASTER. The Scarlet Woman. A poem in six parts by Aleksey Konstantinovich Tolstoy. Part One.
> The merry rev'llers throng the hall;
> The lute plays sweet; the cymbals brawl;
> The crystal blazes; gold shines bright;

> While 'twixt the columns, rich brocades
> Hang swagged with finely broidered braids,
> And flowering shrubs anoint the night . . .

People are listening to him, but from the anteroom come the sounds of a waltz, and the reading stops short. Everyone dances. TROFIMOV, ANYA, VARYA *and* RANYEVSKAYA *emerge from the anteroom.*

RANYEVSKAYA. Now, Petya . . . Petya with the pure soul . . . Please forgive me. Shall we dance . . .? (*Dances with him.*)

ANYA *and* VARYA *dance.*

Enter FIRS. *He puts his stick next to the side door.* YASHA *has also entered, and is watching the dancing.*

YASHA. What's up with you, then, Grandad?

FIRS. I'm not right in myself. When we gave a ball in the old days we used to have generals dancing here, we had barons, we had admirals. Now we send for the postmaster and the station-master, and even them they're none too eager. I'm not as strong as I was. The old master, her grandfather, used to treat all our ailments with a dose of sealing-wax. I've been taking sealing-wax every day for twenty years or more. Maybe that's why I'm still alive.

YASHA. Real old bore, aren't you, Grandad? (*Yawns.*) Why don't you just drop dead?

FIRS. Oh, you . . . sillybilly. (*Mumbles.*)

TROFIMOV *and* RANYEVSKAYA *dance first in the ballroom, and then in the drawing-room.*

RANYEVSKAYA. *Merci.* I'm going to sit down for a moment. (*Sits.*) I'm quite tired out.

Enter ANYA.

ANYA (*excitedly*). Some man just came to the kitchen saying the cherry orchard's been sold.

RANYEVSKAYA. Sold? To whom?

ANYA. He didn't say. He's gone now. (*Dances with* TROFIMOV.)

They both go out into the ballroom.

YASHA. That was just some old man gossiping. Some stranger.

FIRS. And Leonid Andreyich still isn't here. He still hasn't come. He's wearing his light autumn coat, he'll go and catch cold. When will these young people learn?

RANYEVSKAYA. I shall die on the spot. Yasha, go and find out who it was sold to.

YASHA. What, from the old man? He left ages ago. (*Laughs.*)

RANYEVSKAYA (*with slight irritation*). What are you laughing at? What are you so pleased about?

YASHA. Very funny man, that Yepikhodov. Fatuous devil. Old Disasters by the Dozen.

RANYEVSKAYA. Firs, if the estate is sold, where will you go?

FIRS. Wherever you tell me to go.

RANYEVSKAYA. Why are you pulling that face? Are you ill? You could go to bed, you know.

FIRS. Oh, yes . . . (*Smiles.*) I go to bed, and who's going to wait on everyone, who's going to see to everything? There's only me to do the whole house.

YASHA (*to* RANYEVSKAYA). Madam, can I ask you a special favour? If you go to Paris again, please take me with you. I can't possibly stay here. (*Looking round and lowering his voice.*) I don't have to tell you – you can see it for yourself. It's an uneducated country, they're people without any morals. And then on top of that there's the boredom – and the food they give us in the kitchen, it's disgusting – and then there's Firs here wandering round all the time muttering away to himself. Take me with you! Please!

Enter PISHCHIK

PISHCHIK. You wonderful woman, may I beg just one thing? One tiny waltz? (RANYEVSKAYA *accompanies him.*) Enchanting creature! All the same, I shall take a hundred and eighty rubles off you . . . I will, you know . . . (*He dances.*) A hundred and eighty tiny rubles . . .

They have passed through into the ballroom.

YASHA (*sings quietly*). 'And will you know just how my heart beats faster . . .?'

In the ballroom a figure in a grey top hat and check trousers waves its arms and leaps about.

VOICES (*off*). It's Charlotta Ivanovna! Bravo!

DUNYASHA (*who has stopped to powder her nose*). Miss told me to dance because there are too many gentlemen and not enough ladies, and now my head's spinning, my heart's pounding. And the postmaster just told me something that quite took my breath away.

The music becomes quieter.

FIRS. What did he tell you?

DUNYASHA. He said, You're like a flower.

YASHA (*yawns*). The ignorance of these people . . . (*Goes out.*)

DUNYASHA. Like a flower . . . I'm such a sensitive girl – I do terribly love it when people say nice things to me.

FIRS. You'll have your head turned, you will.

Enter YEPIKHODOV.

YEPIKHODOV (*to* DUNYASHA). You've no wish to see me, have you . . . As if I was some kind of insect. (*Sighs.*) Ah, life!

DUNYASHA. What do you want?

YEPIKHODOV. And you're right, no doubt, possibly. (*Sighs.*) Though, of course, if you look at it from one point of view, then I mean you have reduced me – and forgive me for saying this, but I mean I'm not going to mince my words – you have reduced me to, well, let's put it like this, to a complete and utter state of mind. I know what's in my stars – every day some disaster happens – I've long been used to it – I look upon my fate now with a smile. I mean, you gave me your word, and although I . . .

DUNYASHA. Please, we'll talk about it later. Leave me in peace now. I'm busy dreaming. (*Plays with a fan.*)

YEPIKHODOV. Every day another disaster, and I mean, all I do is smile. Laugh, even.

Enter VARYA *from the ballroom.*

VARYA (*to* YEPIKHODOV). Are you still here? Have you no respect? (*To* DUNYASHA.) Out of here, Dunyasha. (*To* YEPIKHODOV.) First you play . billiards and break the cue, and now you parade about the drawing-room as if you were a guest.

YEPIKHODOV. I'm not going to account for my behaviour to you, if I may say so.

VARYA. I'm not asking you to account for your behaviour. I'm telling you. All you do is wander about from place to place. You never get down to any work. We keep a clerk, but what for, heaven only knows.

YEPIKHODOV (*offended*). Whether I do any work or not – whether I wander about or eat or play billiards – these are questions that can only be judged by people older and wiser than you.

VARYA. You dare to talk to me like that! (*Flaring up.*) You dare! Are you trying to tell me I don't know what's right and wrong? Clear off out of here! This minute!

YEPIKHODOV (*cowering*). Kindly express yourself with more refinement.

VARYA (*beside herself*). Out of here! This instant! Out!

He goes to the door, and she after him.

Disasters by the Dozen – that's right! I want neither sight nor sound of you in here!

YEPIKHODOV *is by now out of the room.*

YEPIKHODOV (*off, behind the door*). I'll tell about you!

VARYA. Oh, coming back, are you? (*Seizes the stick that* FIRS *left beside the door.*) Come on, then . . . Come on . . . Come on . . . I'll show you . . . Are you coming? My word, you're going to be for it . . .! (*Raises the stick threateningly.*)

Enter LOPAKHIN.

LOPAKHIN. Thank you kindly.

VARYA (*angrily and sarcastically*). Sorry! My mistake.

LOPAKHIN. That's all right. I'm touched to get such a warm welcome.

VARYA. Oh, please – think nothing of it. (*Goes away from him, then looks round and asks softly.*) I didn't hurt you, did I?

LOPAKHIN. No, no. Don't worry about it. I shall just have the most enormous bump, that's all.

VOICES (*off, in the ballroom*). Lopakhin's arrived! Lopakhin's here!

Enter PISHCHIK.

PISHCHIK. As large as life . . . (*He and* LOPAKHIN *kiss.*) You smell of brandy, my dear fellow. And we're making merry here as well.

Enter RANYEVSKAYA.

RANYEVSKAYA. Is it him . . .? (*To* LOPAKHIN.) Why so long? Where's Leoníd?

LOPAKHIN. He arrived with me – he's just coming . . .

RANYEVSKAYA (*alarmed*). So what happened? Did they hold the sale? Speak!

LOPAKHIN (*confused, afraid to reveal his joy*). The sale ended just on four o'clock. We missed the train – we had to wait till half-past nine. (*Sighs heavily.*) Ouf! My head's rather going round . . .

Enter GAYEV. *In his left hand he is carrying his purchases; with his right he is wiping away his tears.*

RANYEVSKAYA. Lenya! Lenya!, what happened? (*Impatiently in tears.*) Quickly, for the love of God . . .

GAYEV (*gives her no reply except a flap of the hand; to* FIRS, *weeping*). Here, take these . . . anchovies, Crimean herrings . . . I haven't eaten anything all day . . . Oh, what I've been through!

The door into the billiard room is open; the click of balls can be heard.

YASHA (*off*). Seven and eighteen!

GAYEV's expression changes; he is no longer weeping.

GAYEV. I'm horribly tired. Help me change, will you, Firs? (*Goes off to his room by way of the ballroom, with* FIRS *after him.*)

PISHCHIK. What happened at the sale? Tell us!

RANYEVSKAYA. Is the cherry orchard sold?

LOPAKHIN. It is.

RANYEVSKAYA. Who bought it?

LOPAKHIN. I did.

RANYEVSKAYA *is utterly cast down; if she were not standing beside the armchair and the table she would fall.* VARYA *takes the keys off her belt, throws them on the floor in the middle of the room, and goes out.*

I bought it! One moment . . . wait . . . if you would, ladies and gentlemen . . . My head's going round and round, I can't speak . . . (*Laughs.*) We got to the sale, and there was Deriganov – I told you he was going to be there. All your brother had was fifteen thousand, and Deriganov straightway bid the mortgage plus thirty. I thought, all right, if that's the way things are, and I got to grips with him – I bid forty. Him – forty-five. Me – fifty-five. So he's going up in fives, I'm going up in tens . . . Well, that was that. I bid the mortgage plus ninety, and there it stayed. So now the cherry orchard is mine! Mine! (*He gives a shout of laughter.*) Great God in heaven – the cherry orchard is mine! Tell me I'm drunk – I'm out of my mind – tell me it's all an illusion . . . (*Stamps his feet up and down.*) Don't laugh at me!

If my father and grandfather could rise from their graves and
see it all happening – if they could see me, their Yermolay, their
beaten, half-literate Yermolay, who ran barefoot in winter – if
they could see this same Yermolay buying the estate . . . The
most beautiful thing in the entire world! I have bought the
estate where my father and grandfather were slaves, where they
weren't allowed even into the kitchens. I'm asleep – I'm
imagining it – it's all inside my head . . . (*Picks up the keys,
smiling tenderly.*) She threw down the keys – she wants to
demonstrate she's no longer mistress here. (*Jingles the keys.*)
Well, it makes no odds.

    The sound of the band tuning up.

Hey, you in the band! Play away! I want to hear you! Everyone come and watch Yermolay Lopakhin set about the cherry
orchard with his axe! Watch the trees come down! Summer
cottages, we'll build summer cottages, and our grandchildren
and our great-grandchildren will see a new life here . . . Music!
Let's have some music!

    The music plays. RANYEVSKAYA *has sunk down on to a chair
    and is weeping bitterly.*

(*Reproachfully.*) Why, why, why didn't you listen to me? My
poor dear love, you won't bring it back now. (*In tears.*) Oh, if
only it were all over. If only we could somehow change this
miserable, muddled life of ours.

PISHCHIK (*takes him by the arm, speaks with lowered voice*).
She's crying. We'll go next door and let her be on her own.
Come on . . . (*Takes him by the arm and leads him out towards the
ballroom.*)

LOPAKHIN. What's all this? Let's hear that band play! Let's
have everything the way I want it! (*Ironically.*) Here comes the
new landlord, the owner of the cherry orchard! (*Accidentally
bangs into an occasional table, and almost overturns the candelabra.*) I can pay for it all! (*Goes out with* PISHCHIK.)

There is no one in either ballroom or drawing-room except
RANYEVSKAYA, *who sits crumpled and weeping bittterly.*
The music plays quietly.

ANYA *and* TROFIMOV *hurry in.* ANYA *goes up to her mother*
and kneels before her. TROFIMOV *remains by the archway into*
the ballroom.

ANYA. Mama . . .! You're crying, Mama? Dear Mama, sweet,
kind, beautiful Mama – I love you and bless you. The cherry
orchard's sold, it's lost and gone – that's true. But don't cry,
Mama. You still have life in front of you. You still have a
generous heart and a pure soul . . . We'll go away, love, you
and me, we'll go away from here, we'll go away. We'll plant a
new orchard, lovelier still, and when you see it you'll
understand. And your heart will be visited by joy, a quiet, deep,
joy like evening sunlight, and you'll smile again, Mama! Come,
love! Come . . .!

CURTAIN

Act Four

The same as Act One.

There are no curtains at the window, and no pictures. A little furniture remains, stacked up in one corner, as if for a sale. You can feel the emptiness.

Upstage, and by the door leading to the outside, are stacked suitcases, bundles made up for a journey, etc.

The door on the left is open, and the voices of VARYA *and* ANYA *can be heard from beyond.* LOPAKHIN *stands waiting.* YASHA *is holding a tray of glasses filled with champagne.*

In the anteroom YEPIKHODOV *is packing a box. From upstage off can be heard a hum of voices – the peasants who have come to say farewell.*

GAYEV (*off*). Thank you, men. Thank you.

YASHA (*to* LOPAKHIN). The peasants have come to make their farewells. They're a decent enough lot, if you want my opinion. They're just not very bright.

> *The hum of voices dies away.*

> *Enter through the anteroom* RANYEVSKAYA *and* GAYEV. *She is not weeping, but she is pale and her face is trembling. She cannot speak.*

GAYEV. Lyuba, you gave them your purse! You mustn't do things like that! You really must not!

RANYEVSKAYA. I couldn't help it! I simply couldn't help it!

> *They both go out.*

LOPAKHIN (*following them to the doorway*). May I humbly

propose a farewell drink? I didn't think to bring any from town, and I could only find one bottle at the station. Come on – have a drink!

Pause.

What – don't you want to? (*Moves away from the door.*) If I'd known I wouldn't have bought it. Well, I shan't have any, either.

YASHA *carefully places the tray on a chair.*

You might as well have a drink yourself, then, Yasha.

YASHA. To all those departing! And to all those staying behind. (*Drinks.*) This isn't real champagne, I can tell you that.

LOPAKHIN. Eight rubles a bottle.

Pause.

Cold as hell in here.

YASHA. They haven't lit the stoves today. Who cares? We're leaving. (*Laughs.*)

LOPAKHIN. What?

YASHA. Sheer pleasure.

LOPAKHIN. October out there, but the sun's shining, the air's still. It's like summer. Good building weather. (*Glances at his watch, and goes to the door.*) Please bear in mind, ladies and gentlemen, you've only forty-six minutes before the train goes! That means we have to leave for the station in twenty minutes. Do make a little haste, now.

Enter TROFIMOV *from outside, wearing an overcoat.*

TROFIMOV. Just about time to go, isn't it? The carriages are here. Heaven knows where my galoshes are. They've vanished. (*Through the doorway.*) Anya, I haven't got my galoshes! I can't find them!

LOPAKHIN. I have to go to Kharkov – I'll be travelling on the same train as the rest of you. That's where I'm staying all winter. I've just been loafing around all this time with you people, going out of my mind with nothing to do. I can't get by without work. I don't know what to do with my hands. They look strange just hanging around like this. They look as if they belonged to somebody else.

TROFIMOV. Well, in a minute we'll be leaving, and you'll be resuming your valuable labours.

LOPAKHIN. Have a glass.

TROFIMOV. I won't, thank you.

LOPAKHIN. So, you're off to Moscow now?

TROFIMOV. Yes, I'm going into town with them. Then tomorrow morning, on to Moscow.

LOPAKHIN. So what, none of the professors been giving their lectures? All waiting for you to arrive, are they?

TROFIMOV. No business of yours.

LOPAKHIN. How many years now have you been at university?

TROFIMOV. Oh, think up something a bit newer than that. That's an old one – old and feeble. (*Looks for his galoshes.*) Listen, we shall probably never see each other again, so allow me to give you one piece of advice as a farewell present. Don't keep waving your arms about! Break yourself of this habit of gesticulating. And all this business of building summer cottages, then calculating that eventually the people who rent them will turn into landlords themselves – that's also a form of arm-waving. All the same, I can't help liking you. You've got fine, sensitive fingers, like an artist's. You've got a fine, sensitive soul, too.

LOPAKHIN (*embraces him*). Goodbye, then, old son. Thanks for everything. Here – just in case you need it – have some money for the journey.

TROFIMOV. What for? I don't need it.

LOPAKHIN. Look, you haven't got any!

TROFIMOV. Yes, I have. Thank you. I got some for a translation I did. Here, in my pocket. (*Anxiously.*) But what I haven't got is my galoshes!

VARYA (*from the next room*). Take your junk away, will you? (*Throws out on to the stage a pair of galoshes.*)

TROFIMOV. Why are you so cross, Varya? Oh, but these aren't my galoshes!

LOPAKHIN. I planted nearly three thousand acres of poppy this spring, and I've made a clear forty thousand rubles on it. But when my poppy was in bloom – what a picture! So here I am, I'm telling you, I've made forty thousand, and I'm offering you a loan because I've got it there to offer. Why turn up your nose? I'm a peasant . . . I'm not going to tie it up in pink ribbon for you.

TROFIMOV. Your father was a peasant, and mine was a dispensing chemist, and from that follows absolutely nothing at all.

LOPAKHIN *takes out his note-case.*

Leave it, leave it . . . Offer me two hundred thousand if you like, and I still wouldn't take it. I'm a free man. And everything that you all value so highly and dearly – all of you, rich men and beggars alike – it hasn't the slightest power over me. It's just so much thistledown, drifting in the wind. I can manage without you – I can go round the side of you. I'm strong and proud. Mankind is marching towards a higher truth, towards a higher happiness, as high as ever may be on this earth, and I am in its foremost ranks!

LOPAKHIN. And you'll get there, will you?

TROFIMOV. I shall get there.

Pause.

Either get there, or else show others the way.

From the distance comes the sound of an axe thudding against a tree.

LOPAKHIN. Well, then, goodbye, old lad. Time to go. We turn up our noses at each other, you and me, but life goes on regardless. When I'm at work – and I can work long hours and never tire – then my thoughts run easier, and I feel I know why I exist. And how many people are there in Russia, my friend, who exist and never know the reason why? Well, it makes no odds –

it doesn't stop the world going round. I'm told her brother's
found a job – in a bank, apparently – six thousand a year. Only
he'll never stick at it, of course – he's bone idle.

ANYA (*in the doorway*). Mama says will they please not start
cutting down the orchard until she's gone.

TROFIMOV. For heaven's sake – how could anyone have so little
tact? (*Goes out through the anteroom.*)

LOPAKHIN. I'll see to it, I'll see to it . . . It's quite true – these
people . . . (*Goes out after him.*)

ANYA. Has Firs been sent off to the hospital?

YASHA. I told them this morning. I assume they sent him off.

ANYA (*to* YEPIKHODOV, *who is crossing the room*). Ask them, will
you, please, if they've taken Firs to the hospital.

YASHA (*offended*). I told Yegor this morning. What's the point of
asking ten times over?

YEPIKHODOV. The aged Firs, in my considered opinion, is past
repair. It's not a hospital he needs – it's gathering to his fathers.
And I can only envy him. (*Puts down the suitcase he is carrying
on top of a hat-box, and crushes it.*) Of course! Of course! I
knew I was going to do that! (*Goes out.*)

YASHA (*mockingly*). Poor old Disasters!

VARYA (*outside the door*). Have they taken Firs to hospital?

ANYA. Yes, they have.

VARYA. Why didn't they take the letter to the doctor?

ANYA. It'll have to be sent on after him, then. (*Goes out.*)

VARYA (*from the next room*). Where's Yasha? Tell him, will you,
his mother's come. She wants to say goodbye to him.

YASHA (*flaps his hand*). Oh, they'll drive me to drink.

> DUNYASHA *all this while has been busying herself about things;
> now that* YASHA *is alone she goes up to him.*

DUNYASHA. If only you'd just give me a glance, Yasha. You're
going away . . . abandoning me . . . (*Weeps and throws herself
on his neck.*)

YASHA. What's all the crying for? (*Drinks champagne.*) Six days from now I'll be in Paris again. Tomorrow we'll be getting on board that express and we'll be away like smoke. I can't believe it. *Vive la France . . .!* Not my style, this place. I can't live here, there's no help for it. I've seen all I want to see of ignorance – I've had my fill of it. (*Drinks champagne.*) So what's there to cry about? Behave yourself properly, then you won't cry.

DUNYASHA (*powders herself, looking in a little mirror*). You will write to me from Paris, won't you? I loved you, you know, Yasha – I loved you so much! I'm terribly tender-hearted, Yasha!

YASHA. They're coming. (*Busies himself about the suitcases, humming quietly.*)

Enter RANYEVSKAYA, GAYEV, ANYA *and* CHARLOTTA IVANOVNA.

GAYEV. We ought to be going. We haven't much time in hand. (*Looking at* YASHA.) Who is it smelling of herrings?

RANYEVSKAYA. Another ten minutes, and we'll get into the carriages . . . (*Glances round the room.*) Farewell, dear house. Farewell, old grandfather house. The winter will go by, spring will come, and then soon you won't be here – they'll be pulling you down. So many things these walls have seen! (*Fervently kisses her daughter.*) My treasure, you're radiant – your eyes are sparkling like two diamonds. You're pleased, then? Very pleased?

ANYA. Very pleased. There's a new life beginning, Mama!

GAYEV (*cheerfully*). Absolutely – everything's all right now. Before the cherry orchard was sold we were all frightfully upset, we were all suffering. And then, as soon as the question had been finally settled, and no going back on it, we all calmed down, we got quite cheerful even . . . Here am I, I'm an old hand when it comes to banks – and now I'm a financier . . . yellow into the middle pocket . . . and Lyuba, you look better somehow, you really do.

RANYEVSKAYA. Yes. My nerves are better, it's true.

She is helped into her overcoat and hat.

I'm sleeping well. Take my things out, will you, Yasha. It's time to go. (*To* ANYA.) My own little girl, we'll see each other again soon. When I get to Paris I'll be living on the money your great-aunt in Yaroslavl sent to buy the estate – hurrah for her! But it won't last long.

ANYA. Mama, you'll come back soon, soon . . . won't you? I'm going to study and take my examinations – and then I'm going to work, I'm going to help you. Mama, you and I are going to read all sorts of books together. We will, won't we? (*Kisses her mother's hands.*) We'll read in the autumn evenings, read lots and lots of books, and a marvellous new world will open up before us . . . (*Lost in her dreams.*) Come back, Mama . . .

RANYEVSKAYA. I will, my precious. (*Embraces her.*)

Enter LOPAKHIN. CHARLOTTA *quietly hums a tune.*

GAYEV. Charlotta's happy – she's singing!

CHARLOTTA (*picks up a bundle that looks like a swaddled infant*). My little baby! Off to bye-byes now . . .

INFANT (*cries*). Wah! Wah!

CHARLOTTA. Hush, my pretty one! Hush, my darling boy!

INFANT. Wah! Wah!

CHARLOTTA. Poor little thing! (*Tosses the bundle back where it came from.*) So you'll try to find me a place, will you, please? I can't manage otherwise.

LOPAKHIN. We'll find something for you, never you fear.

GAYEV. They're all leaving us. Varya's going away . . . Suddenly no one needs us any more.

CHARLOTTA. I've nowhere to live in town. I shall have to go farther afield. (*Hums.*) But what do I care?

Enter PISHCHIK.

LOPAKHIN. Well, of all the world's wonders . . . !

PISHCHIK (*out of breath*). Oh, let me get my breath back . . . such a state . . . my dear good people . . . water, some water . . .

GAYEV. After money, is he? No good looking at me . . . I shall depart from temptation. (*Goes out.*)

PISHCHIK. Long time since I was in this house . . . wonderful woman . . . (*To* LOPAKHIN.) And you're here . . . Very pleased to catch you . . . Man of enormous intelligence . . . Here . . . Take this . . . Four hundred rubles . . . Eight hundred still to come . . .

LOPAKHIN (*shrugs in bewilderment*). It's like a dream . . . Where on earth did you get it?

PISHCHIK. Wait . . . Hot . . . Most extraordinary thing. Some Englishmen arrived – found some kind of white clay in my land . . . (*To* RANYEVSKAYA.) And four hundred for you . . . You amazing, wonderful woman . . . (*Gives her the money.*) The rest later. (*Drinks the water.*) Someone was just telling me – young man on the train – apparently there's some great philosopher who recommends jumping off the roof. 'Jump!' he says – and apparently that's the whole problem in life. (*In amazement.*) Would you believe it! Some more water . . .

LOPAKHIN. Who were these Englishmen?

PISHCHIK. I gave them a twenty-four year lease on the section with the clay in it . . . But forgive me, I can't stay now . . . I've got to gallop . . . Go and see old Znoykov . . . And Kardamonov . . . I owe money to all of them . . . (*Drinks.*) Your very good health . . . I'll look in on Thursday . . .

RANYEVSKAYA. We're just moving into town – and tomorrow I'm going abroad.

PISHCHIK. What? (*Alarmed.*) What's this about moving into town? So that's why I can see all this furniture . . . all these suitcases . . . Well, there we are . . . (*On the verge of tears.*) There we are . . . People of the most tremendous intelligence, these Englishmen . . . There we are . . . Be happy . . . God give you strength . . . There we are, then . . . To everything in this world there is an end . . . (*Kisses* RANYEVSKAYA's *hand.*) And if one day the rumour reaches you that the end has come for me, then remember this old . . . this old horse, and say: 'Once on this earth there was a certain Simeonov-Pishchik . . . God rest his soul . . .' Most remarkable weather . . . Yes . . . (*Exits in great confusion, but at once returns and speaks from the doorway.*) Dashenka sends her regards! (*Goes out.*)

RANYEVSKAYA. We could even be going now. I'm leaving with two things still on my mind. One is poor Firs. (*Glances at her watch.*) We could wait another five minutes . . .

ANYA. Mama, Firs has been taken to hospital. Yasha did it this morning.

RANYEVSKAYA. My other worry is Varya. She's used to rising early and doing a day's work. Now she has nothing to do all day she's like a fish out of water. Poor soul, she's grown thin and pale, she's forever weeping . . .

Pause.

(*To* LOPAKHIN.) As you well know, I dreamt of . . . seeing her married to you, and everything appeared to be pointing in that direction. (*Whispers to* ANYA, *who motions to* CHARLOTTA, *whereupon both of them go out.*) She loves you – you like her – and why you seem to avoid each other like this I simply do not know. I don't understand it.

LOPAKHIN. I don't understand it myself, I have to admit. It's all very strange. If there's still time, then I'm ready – here and now, if you like. Let's get it over with, and *basta*. I have a feeling I'll never propose once you've gone.

RANYEVSKAYA. Splendid. It'll only take a minute, after all. I'll call her in at once.

LOPAKHIN. We've even got champagne, appropriately enough. (*Looks at the glasses.*) Empty. Someone's drunk the lot.

YASHA *coughs.*

Well, that really is lapping it up.

RANYEVSKAYA (*animatedly*). Wonderful. We'll go out of the room. Yasha, *allez!* I'll call her . . . (*Through the doorway.*) Varya, leave all that and come here. Come on! (*Goes out with* YASHA.)

LOPAKHIN (*looks at his watch*). Yes . . .

Pause.

There is stifled laughter and whispering outside the door. Finally VARYA *comes in.*

VARYA (*looks round the room at some length*). That's strange. I can't find it anywhere . . .

LOPAKHIN. What are you looking for?

VARYA. I packed it myself and I can't remember where.

Pause.

LOPAKHIN. Where are you off to now, then?

VARYA. Me? To the Ragulins. I've agreed to keep an eye on the running of the house for them. Well, to be housekeeper.

LOPAKHIN. That's in Yashnevo, isn't it? What, about forty-five miles from here?

Pause.

Well, here we are, no more life in this house . . .

VARYA (*examining things*). Where is it . . .? Or perhaps I packed it in the trunk . . . No, no more life in this house. Never again.

LOPAKHIN. And I'm off to Kharkov now . . . on this train, in fact. Lot of business to do. I'm leaving Yepikhodov in charge here. I've taken him on.

VARYA. Really?

LOPAKHIN. This time last year we had snow already, if you remember. Now it's calm and sunny. The only thing is the cold. Three degrees of frost.

VARYA. I didn't look.

Pause.

Anyway, our thermometer's broken . . .

Pause.

A VOICE (*through the door from outside*). Where's Lopakhin?
LOPAKHIN (*as if he has been expecting this call for some time*).
Coming! (*Goes rapidly out.*)

VARYA, *now sitting on the floor, lays her head on a bundle of clothing, and sobs quietly. The door opens and* RANYEVSKAYA *cautiously enters.*

RANYEVSKAYA. What?

Pause.

We must go.
VARYA (*she has already stopped crying; wipes her eyes*). Yes, Mama, dear, it's time. I'll get to the Ragulins today provided we don't miss that train . . .
RANYEVSKAYA (*through the doorway*). Anya, get your things on!

Enter ANYA, *followed by* GAYEV *and* CHARLOTTA IVANOVNA. GAYEV *is wearing an overcoat with a hood.*

The SERVANTS *and* CARRIERS *foregather.* YEPIKHODOV *busies himself about the things.*

Well, then, I think we can finally be on our way.
ANYA (*joyfully*). On our way!
GAYEV. My friends! My dear good friends! Leaving this house forever, can I stand silent, can I refrain from saying a word of farewell, from giving expression to those feelings that now invade my whole being . . .?
ANYA (*imploringly*). Uncle!
VARYA. Dear uncle, don't!
GAYEV (*gloomily*). Off the cushion and into the middle . . . I am silent.

Enter TROFIMOV, *followed by* LOPAKHIN.

TROFIMOV. What are we waiting for, then? It's time to go!

LOPAKHIN. Yepikhodov, my coat!

RANYEVSKAYA. I'm going to stop here for one more minute. It's as if I'd never really seen before what the walls in this house were like, what the ceilings were like. And now I look at them avidly, with such a tender love.

GAYEV. I remember, when I was six years old, sitting up on this windowsill on Trinity Sunday and watching my father go to church.

RANYEVSKAYA. Have all the things been taken out?

LOPAKHIN. I think the lot. (*To* YEPIKHODOV, *as he puts on his overcoat.*) Have a look, though, see if everything's all right.

YEPKHODOV (*in a hoarse voice*). Don't worry – leave it to me!

LOPAKHIN. Why are you talking in that sort of voice?

YEPIKHODOV. Just drinking some water, and I swallowed something.

YASHA (*contemptuously*). The ignorance of these people . . .

RANYEVSKAYA. We shall depart, and not a living soul will remain behind.

LOPAKHIN. All the way through until the spring.

VARYA (*pulls an umbrella out of one of the bundles in a way that looks as if she were raising it threateningly :* LOPAKHIN *pretends to be frightened*). What? What are you doing . . .? It never even entered my head.

TROFIMOV. Ladies and gentlemen, we must get into the carriages. It really is time! The train will be arriving any minute!

VARYA. Here they are, Petya – your galoshes, next to this suitcase. (*In tears.*) And what dirty galoshes they are . . .

TROFIMOV (*putting on the galoshes*). Off we go, then!

GAYEV (*in great confusion, afraid of bursting into tears*). The train . . . the station . . . In off into the middle, off the cushion into the corner . . .

RANYEVSKAYA. Off we go!

LOPAKHIN. Are we all here? No one left behind? (*Locks the side door on the left.*) The things are all stacked in here, we must lock up. Right, off we go!

ANYA. Farewell, old house! Farewell, old life!

TROFIMOV. Hail, new life! (*Goes with* ANYA.)

> VARYA *looks round the room and goes out without hurrying.* YASHA *and* CHARLOTTA *go out with her little dog.*

LOPAKHIN. So, until the spring. Out you go, all of you ... Good-bye! (*Goes out.*)

> RANYEVSKAYA *and* GAYEV *are left alone together. As if they have been waiting for this, they throw themselves on each other's necks and sob quietly, restraining themselves, afraid of being overheard.*

GAYEV (*in despair*). My sister, my sister ...

RANYEVSKAYA. Oh my dear orchard, my sweet and lovely orchard! My life, my youth, my happiness – farewell! Farewell!

ANYA (*off, calling cheerfully*). Mama!

TROFIMOV (*off, cheerfully and excitedly*). Hulloooo ...!

RANYEVSKAYA. One last look at the walls ... the windows ... This is the room where our poor mother loved to walk ...

GAYEV. My sister, my sister ...!

ANYA (*off*). Mama!

TROFIMOV (*off*). Hulloooo ...!

RANYEVSKAYA. We're coming!

> *They go out.*

> *The stage is empty. There is the sound of all the doors being locked, and then of the carriages departing. It grows quiet. Through the silence comes the dull thudding of the axe. It sounds lonely and sad. Steps are heard.*

> *From the door on the right comes* FIRS. *He is dressed as always, in jacket and white waistcoat, with his feet in slippers. He is ill.*

FIRS (*goes to the door and tries the handle*). Locked. They've gone. (*Sits down on the sofa.*) They've forgotten about me. Well, never mind. I'll just sit here for a bit . . . And I dare say he hasn't put his winter coat on, he's gone off in his autumn coat. (*Sighs anxiously.*) I never looked to see. When will these young people learn? (*Mutters something impossible to catch.*) My life's gone by, and it's just as if I'd never lived at all. (*Lies down.*) I'll lie down for a bit, then . . . No strength, have you? Nothing left. Nothing . . . Oh you . . . sillybilly . . . (*Lies motionless.*)

A sound is heard in the distance, as if from the sky – the sound of a breaking string, dying away, sad.

Silence descends, and the only thing that can be heard, far away in the orchard, is the thudding of the axe.

CURTAIN

Notes

lvi *She promised to send the money – she gave me some for the journey . . . I was away from home for three weeks . . . All the same, how lovely to spend some time abroad*: in this earlier version of the play Anya is here referring to a visit to the great-aunt (mentioned on p. 19) which is intended by her mother and uncle to elicit money to solve the family's financial problems. The money 'promised' refers to 15,000 roubles, receipt of which is grudgingly acknowledged by Ranyevskaya on p. 41. The money 'for the journey' could be for the journey to Yaroslavl, where the great-aunt lives but, in view of Dunyasha's remark about spending time 'abroad', is more likely to refer to the cost of Anya's trip to Paris, accompanied by Charlotta, when they 'went away in Lent [. . .] in Holy Week' (pp. 4–5), staying there for three weeks before returning with her mother in May when the play commences.
Confusingly, at least one commentator has suggested that Anya has spent the entire five years living abroad with her mother and not just a period of three weeks.

lviii *Weiter!*: 'further' in German, here meaning 'Go on!' (i.e. 'Tell me more').
inside that sack was another sack: the implications are disturbing. Usually one sack or bag would be placed inside another to prevent fluid leaking (e.g. blood from meat). However, whatever is in this receptacle appears still to be alive.

lxi The first, 1904, edition had 'A Comedy in Four Acts' after the title. The Moscow Art Theatre posters described it as 'a drama'. One of the things which Stanislavsky could not accept about *The Cherry Orchard* when he first read it was Chekhov's insistence that it was 'a comedy'. See Translator's Introduction, p. li. Donald Rayfield has pointed out that the title of the play in Russian refers to the sour *vishnia* 'Morello' cherry, which is usually cooked before being eaten, as opposed to the sweet *chereshnia* variety and that, strictly speaking, the play should be called *The Sour-Cherry Orchard* (Rayfield, 1994, p. 136).

lxiii *Ranyevskaya (Lyuba)*: Lyuba is the diminutive of Lyubov which, as well as being a Christian name in Russian also means 'love'. In his correspondence, Chekhov described her as an 'old' woman but, on learning that his wife, Olga Knipper, who was aged thirty-five in 1904, had been cast in the role, he reduced Ranyevskaya's age accordingly but without being specific.

Gayev: a *gaer* (pronounced 'guy-heir' with stress on the second syllable) means 'a buffoon' in Russian. The diminutive form of his name, Lenya (pronounced Lyonya), is short for Leonid. On p. 8 he says he is fifty-one.

Lopakhin: the Russian verb *lopat* means 'to gobble up' (as of food) but may also have metaphorical implications in his case. Chekhov insisted that Lopakhin was not to be played as a crude, boorish individual and had hoped, initially, that Stanislavsky himself would take on the role.

Simeonov-Pishchik: a hyphenated name has similar aristocratic associations for the Russians as it has for the British. In this case it also has comic associations as well in that a *pishchik* is a type of pipe used as a bird lure, or a 'swozzle' used by a puppeteer to produce a comic voice.

Charlotta Ivanovna: Chekhov considered the role of the eccentric governess an important one and proposed Olga Knipper for the part, although Stanislavsky cast her as Ranyevskaya. Her somewhat ambiguous nature is suggested in a letter to Nemirovich-Danchenko in which Chekhov pointed out that the character tends to confuse the masculine and feminine gender of adjectives.

Firs: named after the Orthodox Saint Thyrsus and, despite being an old man, because he is also a servant, referred to familiarly by his Christian name. A point about modes of address which is difficult to bring out in English translation (much easier in French) is the way in which Russians deploy the equivalent of 'thee/thou' and 'you'. The former is normally used between family members, intimate friends and familiar acquaintances but can also be deployed, in particular circumstances, to suggest social superiority or merely to be rude. For example, Lopakhin addresses those he considers his inferiors, such as Yepikhodov and the servants, as 'thou', but he also addresses Pishchik in the same manner (in his case, as someone he considers a friend or social equal). The family, who might be expected to 'thee' and 'thou' their servants, do not do so out of politeness, with the exception of the more conventional Firs who, one might say, expects to be 'thou'd'. Interestingly, the intimacies exchanged between Yasha and Dunyasha are expressed in terms of the more formal 'you', as if basking in the family's politer mode of address to them and seeking to disclaim their actual status as servants.

1   *half-light, shortly before sunrise* [. . .] *May already* [. . .] *Nearly two o'clock*: the fact that it is already getting light at two in the morning would seem to suggest that the play's location is somewhere in central Russia. It also gets very cold as early as October (see p. 55). The estate is forty-five miles from 'Yashnevo' (p. 63), which would appear to be a fictitious place, but the fact that characters in the play travel by train to both Moscow and Yaroslavl helps to give some idea of the play's latitudinal location. Lopakhin also speaks of travelling south to Kharkov in the Ukraine which, at the time, even by train would have taken days rather than hours to reach. He would seem to have business interests in the region, which would probably include the poppy fields referred to on p. 57.

2   *'It'll heal in time for your wedding . . . '*: a common Russian expression of consolation for someone who has hurt him- or herself.
yellow shoes: the shoes are *bashmaki*, high-button boots.
Like a pig in a pastry-cook's . . . : literally 'with a pig's snout in Bakers' Row' – the street in any Russian city market where fine bread and pastries are sold; in other words, out of place or incongruous.
kvass: a sourish drink made from bread, malt and water.
I can't give our climate my seal of approval . . .: Yepikhodov's discourse is characterised by his use, or more often misuse, of high-sounding phrases. This fact is made more obvious in some translations than others.

3   *The stage is empty*: in one sense an unnecessary stage direction but an important one in *The Cherry Orchard*. It is repeated at the end of the play.

4   *(. . . on the verge of tears)*: the stage direction *'skvoz' sliozy'* is more frequently translated as 'through tears' and occurs often in Chekhov's plays. He was at pains to point out that this was not to be taken literally and was merely an indication of tone or mood. See Translator's Introduction, p. lii.

Lent: the period from Ash Wednesday to Easter Eve (forty days) traditionally observed by Christians as a period of fasting and penitence.

5 *He's sleeping in the bath-house*: all Russian estates would have had a *bania*, a kind of sauna or steam room, usually in a hut or cabin separate from the main building and with hot water heated by logs.

Holy Week: the week before Easter Sunday.

6 *Menton*: a coastal resort situated on the French Riviera near Monte Carlo and Nice.

kopeck: the smallest unit of Russian currency; 100 kopecks equal one ruble. It appears as both 'kopeck' and 'kopek' in this translation.

have we paid the interest?: the estate, which is no longer economically viable, has been mortgaged to the bank for a sum of money on which interest has to be paid and, if defaulted upon, the mortgagee's claim to the property then reverts to the bank who, in this case, have decided to sell the estate at auction to the highest bidder.

(looks in at the door, and moos): some translators have 'bleats'. The phonetic indicator in Russian is 'Meh-eh-eh . . . ', suggestive of sheep or, possibly, goats, as well as cattle (see Commentary, p. xli).

7 *an air-balloon*: a form of aerial transport before the invention of the aeroplane and especially associated with the French brothers, Montgolfier. The first-ever flight took place in 1783.

I'd walk all round the holy places: Ranyevskaya has said earlier (p. 4) that Varya looks like a nun. Here she sees herself as a typical pilgrim of the period, travelling on foot from one religious place to another, putting up at monasteries and begging for alms. Kiev and Moscow, capitals of ancient and modern Russia, were also important religious centres.

pippin: ogurchik in the original, literally 'little cucumber', with the implication that Dunyasha is 'a tasty morsel'.

8 *Oh, you sillybilly*: see Commentary, pp. xli–xlii.

post-chaise: the quickest and also an expensive means of travel in the nineteenth century; a light, well-sprung carriage drawn by horses which could be exchanged for fresh ones at regular staging posts.

Oriental-looking trousers: sharovary in the original; broad 'Cossack' trousers tucked into flat-heeled, knee-length boots.

billiards: the Oxford English Dictionary describes billiards as 'a game played with small solid ivory balls on a rectangular table having a smooth cloth-covered horizontal surface, the balls being driven about, according to the rules of the game, by means of long tapering sticks called cues . . . the large table on which the game of billiards is played; usually 12 ft by 6, [is] covered with fine green cloth, surrounded by a cushioned ledge, and provided with six "pockets" at the corners and sides for the reception of the balls.' The game is played with fewer balls than snooker, the object being to gain points by propelling one ball against another to cause a collision or 'cannon' with a third and exploiting the cushioned ledge to achieve this. The Russian variant of the game was apparently played at the time with five balls, one of which was yellow, as opposed to the 'Berlin' variant played with three – one red and two white.

screw back: to strike the cue-ball against another ball in such a way as to cause the cue-ball to travel in reverse.

9   *Who?*: the translation here irons out a characteristic speech 'tic' which Gayev adopts: he invariably says *Chevo?* (Which?) instead of *Chto?* (What?).

scent: 'patchouli' in the original; an East Indian mint-scented perfume.

My beloved child: Ranyevskaya uses a form of address more commonly found in Russian folktales – something like 'cherished child of mine'.

10   *Kharkov*: a large town in the Ukraine about 600 kilometres south of Moscow.

I could throw caution to the winds: *propadai moia telega, vse chetyre kolesa*. Literally, 'May all four wheels fall off my cart', a colloquial expression implying that the speaker is prepared to take a risk and trust in fate while prey to helpless feelings (in this case, of longing). Laurence Senelick suggests that Pishchik is quoting from a folksong here which goes 'lost my cart with all four wheels/lost my heart head over heels' (Chekhov/Senelick, 2006, p. 990).

I want to tell you some very pleasant and cheering news: the exchanges which follow may be said to constitute the heart of the play and the nub of its serio-comic potential. The essential fact which underlies Lopakhin's monologue is that he has money and the estate owners do not. The salvation of the latter is entirely in the hands of the former; all he needs to do is to offer

to lend them the money to pay off their debts. However, he makes any loan conditional on their agreeing to sell the land currently occupied by the orchard for real-estate development. At the same time, he would seem to play down the real value of the land and its potential profitability: ten rubles an acre per year seems a derisory amount (25 rubles per desyatin – 2.5 acres – in the original) while the 25,000-rubles-a-year income he anticipates would seem to underestimate either the acreage per lessee or the number of potential purchasers. Significantly, Lopakhin hints at the possibility of a loan just as he is leaving (p. 14). What he actually says at this point is: '*Ia vzaimy 50,000 dostanu*', which translates literally as 'I'll arrange a loan of 50,000'. What this seems to imply is that he will stand as guarantor for a bank loan which he will secure for the family against an assurance that they will agree to the speculative enterprise he proposes. It is not obvious, at this stage, that he stands to gain anything from the scheme and would appear to be offering disinterested help and advice. However, at the same time, he may well be aware that what he is proposing is not something that the bank is likely to agree to. After all, why should it consider bailing out a group of feckless financial incompetents when it stands to recoup not only what it is owed by them but also to make a substantial profit by selling the estate over the heads of the former owners whose lives are, in an important sense, mortgaged to the bank along with the property? On a more personal level, the bankers can also salve their consciences (recoup their moral losses so to speak) by offering Gayev, who is undoubtedly a social acquaintance of theirs, a job at the bank in recompense (see note to p. 29). In the circumstances, Lopakhin's offer seems almost calculated to be unacceptable. Chekhov once jokingly described himself as a Marxist, when he sold the copyright of his writings to a Russian publisher of the same name (Marks). Nevertheless, the play would seem to contain more than just a hint of the Marxist perception that, as a country (in this case Russia) moves from a society characterised by feudal structures to one based on capitalist norms, relations between people are increasingly reduced to the mechanised level of the cash nexus. In no other play by Chekhov does money play such an important role.
thirteen miles: 'twenty *versts*' in the original; a *verst* is approximately 1,170 yards.

11 *It's a marvellous position with this deep river*: ironically, deep
enough for seven-year-old Grisha to drown in.

Cut it down?: it is interesting to note that, despite the fact that
the emotional attachment of the owners seems to be to the house,
they baulk at the destruction of the orchard rather than the
building. A potential plan for redevelopment might easily retain
the house while selling off the land occupied by the orchard.

You only get a full crop every other year . . . no one buys it:
Stanislavsky records a conversation with Chekhov on semantic
differences connected with the Russian title of the play –
between *Vishnevy sad*, with the stress on the first syllable and
meaning a productive orchard – and *Vishniovy sad*, the play's
actual title, with the stress on the second syllable and
suggestive of an unproductive orchard.

the encyclopaedia: probably the Brockhaus and Efron
encyclopaedia which consisted of eighty-two volumes and four
supplements.

(glances at his watch): a characteristic gesture which suggests
that Lopakhin's preoccupation is constantly with something
beyond the immediate topic of conversation and containing the
possible sense that 'Time is money'.

12 *be fruitful and multiply . . . it may come to pass*: Lopakhin's
expressions have biblical overtones in English which are not
present in the Russian.

*He'll put his couple of acres to some use, and start to cultivate
them*: the comic potential of this remark lies in the fact that the
prospective 'summer countryman' may decide to cultivate
cherry trees on the very spot where the previous trees have
been cut down.

*It's an inanimate object, but all the same, whichever way you
look at it, it's still a bookcase*: the logic of this would seem to
suggest that, on the contrary, it is no longer simply a bookcase,
especially since 'We could celebrate its centenary'. Rather like
Gogol in his novel *Dead Souls* (1842), in *The Cherry Orchard*
Chekhov plays ambiguously with distinctions between
inanimate objects and living people.

14 *Goodbye*: when parting with both Gayev and Pishchik, instead
of using the normal Russian for 'goodbye' (*do svidaniia*)
Lopakhin uses a nonsense expression *do svidansiia*. An English
equivalent might be the pronunciation of the more colloquial
'I'll be seeing you' as 'Abyssinia'.

(Exchanges kisses with Pishchik): it is not unusual for Russian men who know each other well to kiss either on both cheeks or on the lips when meeting or departing.

And my Dashenka . . . she also says: what *does* Dashenka say about Lopakhin? There is the intriguing possibility that Pishchik's off-stage daughter has her sights set on him from the start. Pishchik would also stand to benefit from the match.

The interest on my mortgage is due tomorrow: 'By 1903, almost one-half of all private land in Russia (excluding peasant land) was mortgaged, forcing the landed gentry to sell their estates and join the professional or commercial classes, as Gaev does at the end of the play' (Chekhov/Senelick, 2006, p. 995).

15 *the railway's come through my land*: this was a period of foreign investment – in railways, heavy industry, mining, etc. Just as 'the English' discover china clay on Pishchik's land in Act Four, so probably the Belgians, or some other foreign nationals, have paid money for permission to construct a railway line across his territory.

17 *I'm going to be a perpetual student*: see Translator's Introduction, p. xlix.

gout: a disease, usually hereditary and most often in men, characterised by painful inflammation of the smaller joints, especially the big toe. It is often falsely associated with alcohol consumption.

18 *Yaroslavl*: a town approximately 300 kilometres north-east of Moscow.

19 *a loan against my note of hand to pay the bank interest*: Gayev is being naive if he thinks he can borrow money on the basis of a simple IOU and with little or no security for the loan.

He obviously won't refuse her: Gayev seems to be confident that Lopakhin will give his sister a personal loan, presumably on the basis of sentiment, which again shows how little he understands the business mind.

20 *I am a man of the eighties*: the 1880s in Russia was a period of industrialisation which produced a huge increase in the working-class population. Following the assassination of the more liberal Alexander II, the reign of Alexander III (1882–94) was one of repression and censorship. It was also a period which encouraged foreign investment and which saw the rise of a wealthy class of businessmen. Faced with this, an increasingly marginalised intelligentsia, which had always prided itself on

its humane, liberal outlook, began to gravitate towards radical, populist political movements and even to embrace Marxism. Gayev is suggesting that, as a member of the liberal intelligentsia, he has the interests of 'the people' at heart.

22   *I haven't got proper papers*: all Russians needed an internal passport to permit them to travel freely within their own country. Some groups needed permission both to travel and to live in certain areas. Charlotta's lack of 'proper papers' does not seem to have prevented her from travelling to France and back.

I'd turn somersaults: 'perform the *salto-mortale*' in the original, i.e. death-defying leaps.

23   *'What should I care for life's clamour . . . '*: the opening lines of a popular romantic song.

in full constitution for years: Yepikhodov rather pretentiously attempts to say something like 'fully constitutional', thus implying his cosmopolitan familiarity with the way things are done abroad and vie with Yasha for Dunyasha's attention.

24   *Have you read Buckle?*: pronounced 'Buckley'. Henry Thomas Buckle (1821–62) was an English historian, mostly self-educated, who spoke eighteen foreign languages and amassed an enormous library which helped him compile a monumental *History of Civilization in England* (1857–61) only two volumes of which were published. In these he practised a scientific method of writing history which took into account a country's climate, etc. The two volumes were translated into Russian in 1861 where his materialist approach, which suggested that religion retards the progress of civilisation, appealed to the radicals.

26   *she gives the old men in the kitchen nothing but dried peas*: Varya has denied this earlier (p. 20).

The seventies, the Decadent movement: the 1870s in Russia was a period associated with the so-called *narodniki* (populists) liberal intellectuals who believed that Russia's future lay in opposing capitalist development and the infiltration of Western ideas and, instead, in seeking a more communal type of indigenous social life based on versions of the peasant commune. In pursuit of this, the *narodniki* instituted a kind of people's crusade whereby students and others went to live among the peasants in the hope of both educating them and learning from them. 'The Decadent movement' is another name

for the Russian Symbolists who came to prominence during the
1870s and whose more extreme practitioners were known as
Decadents.

What would it be? A hundred thousand?: interesting to
speculate what might lie behind Lopakhin's question. Having
already mentioned Deriganov's intention to bid for the estate,
could it be that he is worried at the possibility of being outbid
by the owners themselves thanks to their great-aunt's
anticipated generosity? It seems clear that he predicts the likely
selling price to be around 100,000 and has, presumably,
already made up his mind to put in a bid himself.

27 *Just once make up your minds . . .* : it couldn't be clearer. If the
estate owners are prepared to put their aristocratic fastidiousness
aside and become venture capitalists they are 'saved'.

28 *our famous Jewish orchestra*: with 'four fiddles, flute and
double bass' this is a sextet rather than an orchestra and has a
rather unusual make-up. A normal Jewish orchestra would also
contain other wind, as well as percussion instruments and
would have been very popular at weddings.

'Money talks, so here's poor Russkies . . .': a couplet (*kuplet*)
taken from a popular vaudeville of the period. A Russian
vaudeville was a dramatic genre (derived from the French) and
extremely popular during the first half of the nineteenth
century. It was related to comic opera and generally presented
scenes from contemporary life in dialogue which was racy and
often improvised as well as being interspersed with satirical
songs (*kuplety*).

29 *I've been offered a job in a bank*: presumably this happened on
the Tuesday mentioned on p. 19 when Gayev raised the idea of
a loan and was offered a job instead.

30 *I didn't agree to have the Freedom*: Firs is referring to the
Emancipation of the Serfs by Alexander II in 1861, which he
later refers to as 'the troubles' (p. 33).

Now it's all chippety-choppety: '*vrazdrob*' in the original,
which seems to be a word of Firs' own invention but conveys a
sense of being splintered into pieces.

31 *Human pride*: this would seem to be a reference to Gorky's
play *The Lower Depths*, performed at the Moscow Art Theatre
in 1902 (two years before *The Cherry Orchard*), in which a
central character delivers a eulogy to 'Man' about humanity's
reasons for feeling pride in itself and its achievements. In

context, these sentiments are somewhat incongruously placed in the mouth of a down-and-out in a doss-house. Chekhov was an early champion of Gorky's work and encouraged the Art Theatre to stage his plays.

if man is physiologically ill-constructed: this could be construed as a more literate version of Firs' description of himself (and others) as a *'nedotyopa'*.

32   *the intelligentsia*: not 'intellectuals' as such but a distinct section of society consisting of an educated élite who recognise that their privileged position carries with it social responsibilities but who often don't seem to do more than just talk. Trofimov's abuse of 'the intelligentsia' seems misdirected, its real target being aristocratic landowners who behave irresponsibly.

And right in front of their eyes . . . moral squalor: this section was objected to by the censor and had to be rewritten.

thirty and forty to a room: this is not how peasants lived in the countryside. Trofimov is referring to one consequence of the emancipation of the serfs which was the creation of an emergent working class of former peasants who, as Russia pursued industrialisation along Western lines, drifted to the cities in search of work where they began to form an underclass of manual labourers living in the kind of squalid urban conditions which Trofimov describes.

barbarism: *'Aziatchina'* in the original or 'Asianness', i.e. that aspect of the Russian character which owes a debt to their Eastern Tartar ancestry rather than the more 'civilised' West and which is thought to be characterised by violence, drunkenness, slovenliness and torpor.

33   *There goes Yepikhodov*: the previous stage direction and this accompanying moment of speech were absent from the first performance of the play but were subsequently added by Chekhov before publication.

the sound of a breaking string: Chekhov set great store by the importance of the quality of this sound, the source and meaning of which have endless possibilities, ranging from the simple breaking of a guitar string to something more complex and metaphysical. If interpreted as a form of 'sundering', then Firs' talk of its reminding him of the dubious benefits of 'freedom' can be seen to represent disturbing notions of social fragmentation and individual alienation.

34 *A PASSER-BY appears . . . a stolen white-peaked cap*: see A Note on the Translation, pp. lv–lvi. The 'groans' refer to the *burlaki* (barge haulers), whose chant *Ei-niukh-nem* (Yo-heave-ho) was made famous in the 'Song of the Volga Boatmen' and who are depicted in an equally famous painting by Ilya Repin. There is no suggestion in the original that the Passer-by's cap has been 'stolen'.

Now that's enough!: it is worth considering whether Lopakhin's remark is directed at Varya's over-reaction to the Passer-by or at the latter's intrusiveness.

here – ten rubles: at this point, Ranyevskaya gives the Passer-by the amount which Lopakhin suggests can be earned per acre annually from each potential lessee (see p. 11).

35 *Ophelia-Ophoolia*: in the Russian original, Lopakhin calls her *Okhmelia* which echoes the verb *okhmeliat* (to get drunk) and he continues by advising her to 'go to a monastery'. The original line in *Hamlet* is 'Get thee to a nunnery'.

You'll lend me some more won't you?/Your humble servant: it seems clear that Lopakhin is willing to lend trifling amounts but not the sums that really matter.

Nymph in thy orisons . . . dismembered: a misquotation from *Hamlet*, Act III, i. Here the translator has substituted 'dismembered' for 'remembered'. In the Russian original, Lopakhin says 'Okhmelia, oh, nymph, remember me in your prayers', which also mangles the nineteenth-century translation of the play by Nikolai Polevoy.

36 *The possession of living souls*: a 'soul' (*dusha*) has both religious and secular connotations in Russian as it was also the term applied to the peasant serf as a possession, i.e. a landowner might own so many hundred, or thousand, 'souls' on his estate. It is interesting to note that Trofimov, in describing the possession of a living soul as a social evil, is apparently oblivious to its spiritual connotations. The section of this speech from 'They owned living souls' to 'the front hall' was censored because of its political implications and was not restored until 1917.

Have faith in me, Anya . . .: the ending of the act from here on, as it now stands, belongs to the revised first edition of the play. For the original ending to Act Two, see A Note on the Translation, pp. lvi–lviii.

38 *the 'grand-rond'*: a quadrille, which is a dance for an equal number of couples consisting of a group of five country dances

of different rhythms and tempos, originally using folk tunes.
Promenade à une paire!: Promenade (i.e. walk) with your
partner!
Grand-rond balancez . . . !: Reel around and swing your
partners!
Les cavaliers à genoux et remerciez vos dames!: Gentlemen, on
your knees and salute the ladies!
Caligula: 12–41 AD (Roman Emperor 37–41 AD); real name
Gaius but nicknamed Caligula because of the small military
boots (*caligae*) he wore as a child. As a result of an illness
which appears to have left him deranged he married his sister,
then murdered her, claimed to be a god and tried to have his
horse elected a consul. After four years of wilful and
inconsistent rule he was murdered by members of his own
guard.

39 *Nietzsche*: German philosopher (1844–1900), best known for
his notion of the '*übermensch*' (the superman). His ideas were
highly influential in Russia at the turn of the century and,
among other things, challenged conventional morality.
the lezghinka: a lively Caucasian dance in two-four time
popularised by the Russian composer Mikhail Glinka
(1804–57).
The sale probably never took place: the point at which the
audience realises that these incongruous celebrations are taking
place on 22 August, the day of the auction.

40 *Ein, zwei, drei!*: 'One, two, three!' in German.
Yes, I've rather taken a fancy to you: in the original, Charlotta
says something like 'You, madam, have also appealed to me'
and, in the process, confuses her genders by using the
masculine form of the verb.
Guter Mensch, aber schlechter Musikant: 'A good man, but a
poor musician' – a line from the German comedy *Ponce de
Leon* (1804) by Clemens von Brentano, meaning a person of
modest artistic abilities. In this case, it has other more
suggestive connotations.

41 *They've thrown you out of university*: Chekhov made it clear
in a letter to Olga Knipper that Trofimov has been thrown out
of university for political reasons, not for wasting time or for
intellectual weakness.

45 *The Scarlet Woman*: '*Greshnitsa*' in the original (The Sinful
Woman). See A Note on the Translation, p. lv.

Tolstoy: A.K. Tolstoy (1817–75), poet and writer of historical dramas, not to be confused with the novelist Leo Tolstoy (no relation). The poem is not given verbatim in the original text.

46 *I've been taking sealing-wax*: a remedy in which sealing-wax is ground, dissolved in hot water and drunk.
Merci: 'thank you' in French.

48 *'And will you know just how my heart beats faster . . . ?'*: '"Wilt thou learn my soul's unrest . . ." Title and opening line of a ballad by N.S. Rzhevskaya (1869).' (Chekhov/Senelick, 2006, p. 1026).

51 VARYA *. . . throws [the keys] on the floor . . . and goes out*: just at the point where Varya should realise where her best interests lie, she betrays her real feelings and simultaneously ruins any future possibility of marriage to Lopakhin.

51 *the cherry orchard is mine! . . . The most beautiful thing in*
-2 *the entire world!*: the irony of course is the fact that, having acquired the orchard, he intends to destroy it.

52 *will see a new life here*: Lopakhin's version of what constitutes a 'new life' may be said to contrast with that of Anya (p. 59) and Trofimov (p. 66).
Accidentally bangs into an occasional table, and almost overturns the candelabra: an indicator of his tipsiness.

55 *galoshes*: rubber overshoes.

57 *I planted nearly three thousand acres of poppy . . . forty thousand roubles*: poppy seed has always been a common ingredient in Russian cookery, especially in bread and cake-making. However, this is a mere by-product of poppy-growing and would not be the economic reason for large-scale cultivation. There are over 400 species of poppy, the most infamous variety of which is *papaver somniferum* from which opium and heroin are derived. Poppy cultivation on this scale would usually be for the purpose of growing opium poppies whose pods could be used for beneficial purposes as sleep aids and painkillers and would have been used in hospitals at the time as an anaesthetic. However, there are also other less beneficial aspects to their cultivation. It is interesting that Chekhov specifies poppies rather than, say, a more conventional agricultural product. The point here would seem to be that Lopakhin is indifferent to the uses to which the crop is put so long as it makes a lot of money. Trofimov has just described him as a 'sensitive soul', and Lopakhin certainly

seems capable of appreciating the aesthetic beauty of the poppies just as he appreciates the beauty of the orchard, but it is the cash value of each which is primary, irrespective of moral or aesthetic considerations. There is, therefore, the possibility that the crop might be bought by dealers who exploit its possibilities as an addictive drug. As a doctor, Chekhov knew all about the uses and abuses of dangerous drugs. His nephew, Kolia, became addicted to opium; the eponymous anti-hero in *Uncle Vanya* steals morphine (a derivative of opium) when threatening suicide, while Chekhov himself took opium to ease chronic chest pains during the last months of his illness. Commentators have tended to gloss over or ignore the ambivalent connotations of this moment in the text.

Mankind is marching towards a higher truth: these sentiments, or similar ones, seem to belong to a character from a play by Gorky rather than Chekhov and are recognisable as typical clichés of later Soviet literature composed according to 'socialist realist' norms.

58 *Has Firs been sent off to hospital? . . . Yes, they have*: note how Anya is assuming that Firs has been sent off to hospital but Yepikhodov hasn't yet confirmed it.

The aged Firs . . . is past repair: a fairly cynical sentiment in the mouth of someone like Yepikhodov but one which picks up on the idea of a *nedotyopa* – something, or someone in this case, broken or worn out – perhaps because 'poorly made' in the first place.

59 *Vive la France!*: Long live France!

60 *I'll be living on the money your great-aunt in Yaroslavl sent to buy the estate*: Ranyevskaya's 'aristocratic' attitude towards money includes both her capacity to reward a vagrant with a gold coin but also, casually, to misappropriate other people's money at will.

I'm going to study and take my examinations – and then I'm going to work, I'm going to help you: the implication is that Anya will remain in the district under her uncle's protection while continuing her education, in the expectation that her mother will return to Russia once the great-aunt's money has run out – at which point Anya will work to support her. There is no suggestion that Anya will leave with Trofimov for Moscow, although that is how the final scene of the play is often interpreted.

(Tosses the bundle back where it came from): given the
carelessness with which people are treated in this play, on a par
with objects, perhaps Charlotta's initial cradling of the bundle
followed by its careless dispatch can be linked metaphorically
with Grisha's drowning, on a par with Ranevskaya's tendency
throughout the play either to drop things or mislay them.
Charlotta's own fate is unclear. Lopakhin says he'll 'find
something for her' while she herself says she'll have to 'go
farther afield' but doesn't seem to care what happens to her.
They're all leaving us: in the original, Gayev's remark would
seem to have a closer link with Charlotta's action: '*Vse nas
brosaiut*' ('They're all abandoning us' or, more literally,
'They're all throwing us away').

61 *some great philosopher*: Pishchik would seem to be referring to
the views on suicide of the German philosopher Artur
Schopenhauer (1788–1860) who, in his *The World as Will and
Representation* (vol. 1, 1819; vol. 2, 1844) declared that 'Far
from being denial of the will, suicide is a phenomenon of the
will's strong affirmation' (vol. 1, trans. E.F.J. Payne, New
York, 1969, p. 398). The only contemporary to have actually
devoted an entire work to the study of suicide was the French
sociologist, Emile Durkheim, in 1897, but he did not
recommend jumping off roof tops.

62 *Firs has been taken to hospital*: he hasn't, of course, and given
that he is, apparently, her first concern it is surprising that
Ranyevskaya simply proceeds to her second concern without
asking why nobody has informed her of Firs' departure. Nor
does she express regret at not having said goodbye when she is
never likely to see him again.
basta: enough (Italian).

62 Commentators are struck by Chekhov's frequent references
–3 to Shakespeare's *Hamlet*. Ranyevskaya's contriving of the
scene between Varya and Lopakhin would seem to cast her in
the role of Polonius in 'loosing' her adopted daughter on the
businessman (see *Hamlet*, II, ii), a scene which is followed by
the one between Hamlet and Ophelia referred to by Lopakhin
on p. 35.

63 *allez!*: go [away] (French).

65 *I'm going to stop here for one more minute*: it is a Russian
custom to sit down for a moment before departure, on the
luggage if nothing else is available, which is probably what

Ranyevskaya is doing at this point.

Trinity Sunday: the Sunday closest to fifty days after Easter in the Russian Orthodox Church calendar.

I swallowed something: perhaps Yepikhodov's worst imaginings, of swallowing a cockroach, have come about (see p. 24).

Questions for Further Study

1. How is the relationship between the sexes presented in *The Cherry Orchard*?
2. How is the relationship between generations portrayed in *The Cherry Orchard*?
3. How important is the past, and especially childhood, for the present behaviour of the characters in *The Cherry Orchard*?
4. How important a role does Charlotta play in *The Cherry Orchard*?
5. Consider the significance of roles performed by off-stage characters in *The Cherry Orchard*, who are referred to but who never appear.
6. What part does the depiction of the natural world, including the orchard itself, play in *The Cherry Orchard*?
7. Chekhov is considered a master of mood and atmosphere. How is a sense of mood (or changes of mood) evoked in Act Two from the point where Gayev addresses the setting sun to the entry of the passer-by and how would you define its/their nature? Alternatively, consider the same question in relation to Act Three from the moment of Lopakhin's entry to the end of the act.
8. What kind of importance do personal idiosyncrasies (usually of a physical kind such as arm-waving, dropping things, falling over things, practising billiard strokes, etc.) play in *The Cherry Orchard*?
9. The action of the *The Cherry Orchard* appears to consist of a series of arrivals and departures, the briefest being 'There goes Yepikhodov . . .' in Act Two. What is the overall effect of this strategy?
10. Consider the importance of sound effects in *The Cherry Orchard* and, especially, the significance of the sound of the 'breaking string'.

11. Chekhov has been described as a forerunner of the so-called 'Theatre of the Absurd'. How far do you think *The Cherry Orchard* serves to explain, or even justify, this link?

12. Soviet interpretations of *The Cherry Orchard* tended to see it as a play about dispossession of the aristocracy by a rising merchant class, with revolutionary events, anticipated by Trofimov, in the near future. To what extent would you support this kind of historical/sociological reading of the play?

13. As the grandchild of a former serf, Chekhov might be said to have been particularly aware of social divisions in the Russian society of his day. To what extent does this awareness find expression in *The Cherry Orchard*?

14. In response to Stanislavsky's description of *The Cherry Orchard* as a moving tragedy, Chekhov insisted that it was a comedy, even at times a farce. Whose view do you think was the more apposite and why?

15. Given the apparent emphasis in the last act on a future and a new life for everyone, why do you think Chekhov chooses to conclude the play in the way he does?

16. Some Russian Symbolists who were contemporaries of Chekhov described *The Cherry Orchard* as 'a puppet show overshadowed by horror'. What do you think they meant and did they have a case?

17. To what extent are references to money an important element in understanding the play's significance?

18. Consider the nature and function of stage furniture and stage properties in *The Cherry Orchard*.

19. What is the effect of the proliferation of ellipses (i.e. '. . .' at the end of sentences or phrases) and how might it affect a performance of *The Cherry Orchard* as a whole or any particular section of it?

20. Bearing in mind that Stanislavsky was the first director of *The Cherry Orchard*, what kind of production method(s) best suit the type of play you take it to be?

21. Do you think the original ending to Act Two of *The Cherry Orchard* should be restored? Give grounds for your reasons.

Bloomsbury Methuen Drama Student Editions

Jean Anouilh *Antigone* • John Arden *Serjeant Musgrave's Dance*
Alan Ayckbourn *Confusions* • Aphra Behn *The Rover* • Edward Bond
Lear • *Saved* • Bertolt Brecht *The Caucasian Chalk Circle* • *Fear and
Misery in the Third Reich* • *The Good Person of Szechwan* • *Life of Galileo* •
Mother Courage and her Children • *The Resistible Rise of Arturo Ui* • *The
Threepenny Opera* • Anton Chekhov *The Cherry Orchard* • *The Seagull* •
Three Sisters • *Uncle Vanya* • Caryl Churchill *Serious Money* • *Top Girls*
• Shelagh Delaney *A Taste of Honey* • Euripides *Elektra* • *Medea*•
Dario Fo *Accidental Death of an Anarchist* • Michael Frayn *Copenhagen*
• John Galsworthy *Strife* • Nikolai Gogol *The Government Inspector* •
Robert Holman *Across Oka* • Henrik Ibsen *A Doll's House* • *Ghosts*•
Hedda Gabler • Charlotte Keatley *My Mother Said I Never Should* •
Bernard Kops *Dreams of Anne Frank* • Federico García Lorca *Blood
Wedding* • *Doña Rosita the Spinster* (bilingual edition) •*The House of
Bernarda Alba* • (bilingual edition) • *Yerma* (bilingual edition) • David
Mamet *Glengarry Glen Ross* • *Oleanna* • Patrick Marber *Closer* • John
Marston *Malcontent* • Martin McDonagh *The Lieutenant of Inishmore* •
Joe Orton *Loot* • Luigi Pirandello *Six Characters in Search of an Author*
• Mark Ravenhill *Shopping and F***ing* • Willy Russell *Blood Brothers*
• *Educating Rita* • Sophocles *Antigone* • *Oedipus the King* • Wole
Soyinka *Death and the King's Horseman* • Shelagh Stephenson *The
Memory of Water* • August Strindberg *Miss Julie* • J. M. Synge *The
Playboy of the Western World* • Theatre Workshop *Oh What a Lovely
War* Timberlake Wertenbaker *Our Country's Good* • Arnold Wesker
The Merchant • Oscar Wilde *The Importance of Being Earnest* •
Tennessee Williams *A Streetcar Named Desire* • *The Glass Menagerie*

Bloomsbury Methuen Drama World Classics

include

Jean Anouilh (two volumes)
Brendan Behan
Aphra Behn
Bertolt Brecht (eight volumes)
Büchner
Bulgakov
Calderón
Čapek
Anton Chekhov
Noël Coward (eight volumes)
Feydeau (two volumes)
Eduardo De Filippo
Max Frisch
John Galsworthy
Gogol
Gorky (two volumes)
Harley Granville Barker
 (two volumes)
Victor Hugo
Henrik Ibsen (six volumes)
Jarry

Lorca (three volumes)
Marivaux
Mustapha Matura
David Mercer (two volumes)
Arthur Miller (six volumes)
Molière
Musset
Peter Nichols (two volumes)
Joe Orton
A. W. Pinero
Luigi Pirandello
Terence Rattigan
 (two volumes)
W. Somerset Maugham
 (two volumes)
August Strindberg
 (three volumes)
J. M. Synge
Ramón del Valle-Inclán
Frank Wedekind
Oscar Wilde

Bloomsbury Methuen Drama Contemporary Dramatists
include

John Arden (two volumes)
Arden & D'Arcy
Peter Barnes (three volumes)
Sebastian Barry
Dermot Bolger
Edward Bond (eight volumes)
Howard Brenton
 (two volumes)
Richard Cameron
Jim Cartwright
Caryl Churchill (two volumes)
Sarah Daniels (two volumes)
Nick Darke
David Edgar (three volumes)
David Eldridge
Ben Elton
Dario Fo (two volumes)
Michael Frayn (three volumes)
David Greig
John Godber (four volumes)
Paul Godfrey
John Guare
Lee Hall (two volumes)
Peter Handke
Jonathan Harvey
 (two volumes)
Declan Hughes
Terry Johnson (three volumes)
Sarah Kane
Barrie Keeffe
Bernard-Marie Koltès
 (two volumes)
Franz Xaver Kroetz
David Lan
Bryony Lavery
Deborah Levy
Doug Lucie

David Mamet (four volumes)
Martin McDonagh
Duncan McLean
Anthony Minghella
 (two volumes)
Tom Murphy (six volumes)
Phyllis Nagy
Anthony Neilsen (two volumes)
Philip Osment
Gary Owen
Louise Page
Stewart Parker (two volumes)
Joe Penhall (two volumes)
Stephen Poliakoff
 (three volumes)
David Rabe (two volumes)
Mark Ravenhill (two volumes)
Christina Reid
Philip Ridley
Willy Russell
Eric-Emmanuel Schmitt
Ntozake Shange
Sam Shepard (two volumes)
Wole Soyinka (two volumes)
Simon Stephens (two volumes)
Shelagh Stephenson
David Storey (three volumes)
Sue Townsend
Judy Upton
Michel Vinaver
 (two volumes)
Arnold Wesker (two volumes)
Michael Wilcox
Roy Williams (three volumes)
Snoo Wilson (two volumes)
David Wood (two volumes)
Victoria Wood